W9-AEU-445

THE GARDEN PACK

SUE PHILLIPS

WITH ILLUSTRATIONS BY IAN SIDAWAY

VIKING

CONTENTS

HOW TO USE THIS PACK   4

WORKING OUT WHAT YOU WANT 6

STARTING TO DESIGN   8

CHOOSING PLANTS   10

BASIC PLANS   12

SHADY SPOTS   14

HOT SUNNY SITUATIONS   16

WET CLAY SOIL   18

DRY SANDY SOIL   20

ACID SOIL   22

CHALKY SOILS   24

SLOPING SITES   26

WINDY EXPOSED SITES   28

FAMILY GARDEN   30

SECURITY   32

LOW MAINTENANCE GARDEN   34

YEAR-ROUND INTEREST   36

PLANT DIRECTORY   38

HOW TO USE THIS PACK

Very few gardeners have the knack of visualizing how a planned garden will look. The Garden Pack changes this, by letting you experiment with the full range of garden features until you achieve the ideal garden.

This pack contains:

🍃 *Thirteen sheets representing grass, gravel, bricks, granite setts, paving, and water that can be cut to the desired shapes.*

🍃 *More than 265 full color, self-standing plant cards representing trees, shrubs, climbers, flowers, and ground cover. Each plant is labeled on the back for immediate identification. Simply press out each plant you require and insert it into its stand. You can create extra plants by color photocopying the cards or making your own from magazine cut-outs or seed catalogs.*

At the back of this book are the vital statistics, a listing of the 265 plants contained in the pack, detailing their soil and climate requirements, whether they like sun or shade, and the height to which they will grow.

A fold-out base board with a printed grid so you can design to scale. One square equals 1 square foot.

The boundaries—brick walls, hedges, and fences—are also self standing.

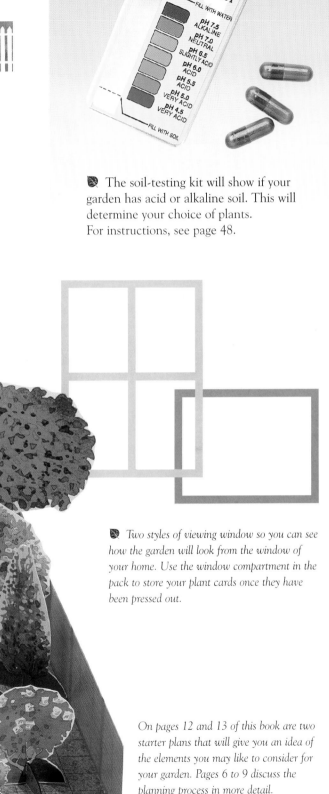

The soil-testing kit will show if your garden has acid or alkaline soil. This will determine your choice of plants. For instructions, see page 48.

Two styles of viewing window so you can see how the garden will look from the window of your home. Use the window compartment in the pack to store your plant cards once they have been pressed out.

On pages 12 and 13 of this book are two starter plans that will give you an idea of the elements you may like to consider for your garden. Pages 6 to 9 discuss the planning process in more detail.

WORKING OUT WHAT YOU WANT

Whether you are starting with a bare plot, or converting a secondhand one full of existing features, the biggest problem in designing a garden is knowing where to start. The main advantage of starting on paper is that you can try out different ideas and judge the effect before committing yourself. Take your time, invent several completely different schemes, play with different ideas, and then choose which you like best.

The garden should reflect something of the style of the house that goes with it. Here, a formal pond and fountain surrounded by steps and flower beds create a small garden with a faintly traditional air, that would look well with an older property. The impatiens (patience plants) filling the flower beds are useful for giving a good show of color in a garden that is in shade for much of the day.

When you eventually have a design you are happy with, make a paper plan you can keep and refer to later, as the work progresses. (Most people make their garden in several stages as time and money allow).

At each stage it is possible to make alterations to the original design so there is no need to feel that, when made, a garden plan can never be changed. Start by making a list of what you want from the garden. Don't worry if this seems very basic—things like somewhere to relax in the sun, lots of scent and flowers, privacy from neighbors, a few herbs and salad greens to pick in summer, a place for pets and children to play.

Put them in order of importance to help you set your priorities. Think about how much time you have for gardening on a regular basis. If you are happy to spend a whole day each weekend during the summer, you could have a rather elaborate garden, but if low-maintenance is essential, then you should plan for it.

How about cost? Will it be more effective to spend a little more money on a few large, impressive, space-filling plants instead of a tapestry of small ones?

Assess the site. Which areas are sunny and which in shade? Add a compass rose to your plan showing north and south—this will give a good idea of which areas will be in sun and which in shade, and for how much of the day.

Is the soil wet clay, dry sand, or acid—or just normal soil in which most things grow? Local garden centers, garden clubs, or experienced gardeners can probably tell you if you don't know.

What is the style of the house? This may suggest that you plan a formal garden, all straight lines, or a more natural one based on loose curves.

Don't forget practical things too. Do you need somewhere to conceal garbage cans and an oil tank, make compost, or store garden tools, outdoor furniture, and barbecue equipment in winter? What access is needed to doorways, garden gates, or the

This rather formal layout with double border and gravel path is both a pretty and practical solution for a small plot. The gravel path is harder wearing than a small lawn, which would turn muddy in wet weather. (There is also no need to buy and store a lawn mower). The mixed borders and backbone of clipped evergreens between them provide something of interest all year round.

GROWING CONDITIONS

🍃 **Light** – sun/half sun/partial shade/shade
full sun = sun all day, half sun = in sun for about half the day
partial shade = dappled shade under a light canopy of trees or
shrubs, shade = no direct sun but not so dark you can't read

🍃 **Soil pH**
acid/normal/chalky acid = pH 4.4-6.0
slightly acid = pH 6.5
neutral = pH 7
alkaline = ph 7.5 upwards

🍃 **Soil type** – sandy/normal/clay
sandy soil feels gritty when rubbed between fingers
normal soil is usually dark especially if it has been well cultivated
clay soil feels sticky and smears on hands when wet

🍃 **Drainage** – fast drying/normal/wet
fast drying soil = puddles vanish within an hour of rain
normal soil = puddles last a few hours
wet soil = puddles remain for days

CHECKLIST

- 🌱 Your requirements
- 🌱 Existing features
- 🌱 Budget
- 🌱 Soil type
- 🌱 Storage space
- 🌱 Maintenance time
- 🌱 House style
- 🌱 Routes

A good garden for people with little time to spare. The style is loosely based on minimalist oriental gardens, using a very few plants chosen to look good grouped together, plus a few rocks and gravel path. The result is a low-maintenance garden that has a tranquil ambience. The plants used are typical of oriental gardens– Japanese maple (Acer palmatum), rhododendron, camellia, and bamboo, with plenty of other evergreens for year-round effect.

An enthusiast's garden–a more complicated design for the keen water gardener who wants a style that gives plenty of scope for fulfilling their hobby. The central pond, which replaces a lawn in a more conventional garden, will need a certain amount of routine work, though the borders will be relatively low-maintenance–specially if well mulched each spring–as they rely mainly on shrubs and herbaceous plants. Moisture-loving kinds such as ligularia and hosta add to the waterside feel, though there is a reasonable sprinkling of evergreens such as bamboo to maintain interest in winter.

garage, etc? People will always take the quickest route, stepping over flower beds, or even walking through them if there is no path.

Use the guidelines in this booklet to help you formulate ideas, then use the three-dimensional garden and stand-up plant cards in the pack to try out different combinations and judge the effect. But start each new idea based on your own set of needs, plus existing features you can't change—such as big trees—and those you want to keep, such as particular shrubs or a border. The easy way to make sure you don't forget them is to make a large-scale plan of the garden on squared paper and mark these features. Also mark the position of doors and windows opening onto the garden, so that you have clear walkways from the front or back door to garden gates or the garage, as well as a good view from each of the windows. Now you are ready to start designing your garden.

STARTING TO DESIGN

Gardens consist of three main ingredients: soft surfaces like grass, hard surfaces like paths and paving, and the plants themselves. The proportions will vary from one type of garden to another and these will affect the amount of maintenance needed later. The shapes of these three elements will form the basis of the garden design.

Too often people will simply run a border bed around the edge of the garden and leave a square or oblong of lawn in the middle. But it is much more interesting to have a round lawn, or to use two overlapping shapes—perhaps a circle or a square—of different sizes.

Even the tiniest town garden can be transformed by good design; here, wooden decking and a mixture of contrasting foliage plants provide low-maintenance plus year-round interest. Due to high surrounding walls, shade-loving plants have been selected, including hardy ferns, euonymus, hosta, ivies, aucuba, and Japanese maple.

Even in a small garden, it is a good idea to include a "secret" area that cannot be seen from the house, to encourage you to go out and discover what lies beyond. Some gardens use gateways or arches to suggest an illusion of space that may not be there at all—what looks like an entrance may lead nowhere.

CHECKLIST

❧ Hard *v.* soft surfaces

❧ Basic outlines

❧ Hard (stone or concree) features

❧ Plants

❧ Alternatives

If the garden is an oddly-shaped plot—perhaps long and narrow, or even L-shaped—then it is much easier to divide it up into several smaller areas instead of treating it as one large space. A series of garden "rooms" will not only look good, they are also fashionable and make it easy to fit in large numbers of plants. When the basic shape of the garden is decided, the next step is to add features like paving, paths, ponds, or borders.

Remember the basic principles; paths should be laid where people need to go, ponds must be in a sunny spot well away from trees or hedges that will shed leaves into them, and paved areas are usually best in a sunny sheltered spot surrounded by walls for privacy.

Deciding on individual plants is the last step—the window dressing. If you want to practice, use this basic garden plan to try out a few ideas. The same shape can be adapted to create all sorts of different gardens, simply by filling in the basic shapes with different ingredients.

Short of ideas? Don't be afraid to look at pictures in books and magazines, or visit other people's gardens for inspiration. And if you run out of plants or surfaces from the garden pack kit, cut out pictures from seed and plant catalogs or magazines, and use colored plain paper to represent gravel or grass.

Very formal, symmetrical gardens are once again fashionable. A design such as this looks striking, yet is quick and easy to maintain since there is no lawn and the beds are narrow and easy to work on. The dwarf box edging occupies much of the bed space, leaving only a relatively small area to be replanted with bedding in spring and fall; this and the evergreen planting against the rear wall mean the garden looks good all year round.

A conventional garden of lawn surrounded by borders has been given a different treatment here simply by altering the shape of the lawn, which distracts attention from the regular shape of the plot and makes the whole garden suddenly far more interesting. Yet the area devoted to borders remains small, so maintenance is quick and easy.

CHOOSING PLANTS

Using plants to fill in the spaces on a garden plan marked "beds" or "borders" isn't quite as simple as an artist using paint to color a picture. Plants are living things with individual requirements. If they are planted in the wrong conditions, they will never do well, however wonderful the garden design may be. Fortunately there are lots of easy-going plants that will grow in most reasonable conditions; some are fussier and need sun or shade, others must have acid soil or free-draining ground where puddles don't hang around after rain. Plants also vary in shape, size, and speed of growth, and each has its own special characteristics that earn it a place in the garden. Without taking years to become a plant expert, it is possible to use plants to "decorate" a garden just by doing a little basic research first.

Hardy cranesbills (Geranium species) are useful go-anywhere plants for creating colorful ground cover in light shade under shrubs. A dense carpet of cranesbills, with underlying bark mulch, is a decorative and useful way of smothering weeds. Visually, they also help to "pull together" the group of larger plants nearby. This is Geranium erianthum, but a wide range of species is available.

Herbaceous plants need a sunny situation with good, fertile, but reasonably well-drained soil to thrive. The trick of making a herbaceous border look good is to place plants with contrasting shapes next to each other. Team spiky shapes with frothy flowers and upright foliage with leafy domes and ground cover. Use the foliage of those plants not in flower to separate blocks of color to make better

Plants in most garden centers come complete with labels that include a color picture, an idea of ultimate shape and size, together with details of any special conditions, such as sun, shade, or soil. Make a preliminary visit or check in a book—265 good basic plants are listed on pages 38–47, along with their vital statistics. Match plants to your own site conditions: list suitable kinds from which to select as you fill in your plan. When making a planting plan, start with the plants that create the biggest effect—trees and evergreen shrubs. These form the year-round backbone shape of the garden. Next, add smaller plants such as small shrubs and herbaceous flowers. Leave the very smallest plants until last. The effect of a bed of alpines or mixed bedding is not achieved by the individual plants, but by the massed impression.

When you come to the fine detail of choosing plants to put next to each other, a good general rule is to select those with contrasting shapes and textures. Mix upright with low spreading plants, large round leaves with erect spiky shapes, tubular flowers with small frothy ones. It is very easy to test how different plants look together in a garden center, by simply lifting out potted plants and standing them next to each other. When you have several groups of plants that look good together, they can quite easily be joined visually by using a fairly bland carpeting plant to make a complete border.

Foliage creates a much longer-lasting effect in the garden than flowers so, when planning a display, try to choose plants with good foliage that will also look good outside their flowering season. Grasses, gold or variegated forms of popular plants, and plants with large, architecturally shaped leaves are especially valuable. Pulmonaria, variegated comfrey, brunnera, and golden birch are all useful.

CHOOSING PLANTS

❧ Eventual size

❧ Shape

❧ Character

❧ Special attractions

❧ Workload

GROWING CONDITIONS

❧ Light (sun, part sun, or shade)

❧ Soil pH level (acid, normal, or alkaline)

❧ Soil type (sandy, normal, or clay)

❧ Drainage (fast drying, normal, or wet)

Conifers come in many shapes, sizes, colors, and textures, making them easy to use when creating striking plant groupings. Team tall pillar shapes with dome and flame shapes and use low spreading kinds like Juniperus squamata "Blue Carpet" as ground cover around them. Neighboring plants need similarly strong shapes and colors like the striking Acer palmatum "Dissectum Garnet," shown here. Heaths, grasses, and low, carpet-forming evergreens are other good choices.

BASIC PLANS

The basic garden shape is the most important single part of a garden design. But the character of the garden depends on the actual plants used—the same basic layout can be given an entirely different style by using different types of plants. The plan shown here is a very versatile one that could easily form the basis of a family garden, low-maintenance garden, cottage garden, or even a fairly formal garden, depending on how it is "decorated." This is a useful point to bear in mind if you are designing a garden where you anticipate needing to make changes over the years, as for instance a family garden whose basic "bones" (features like paving, or trees) are then used later as the main structure of a different garden intended as an absorbing hobby for the parents in later life.

COTTAGE GARDEN

Cottage gardens are enthusiasts' gardens, where the main requirement is to provide plenty of space to grow a big range of plants—lawns scarcely figure, and even paving has low plants such as scented herbs growing in the cracks between slabs. Although a traditional cottage garden centers around flowers and roses, some other shrubs have also been included to give a longer season of interest—choose those with fruit or blossom-like flowers for a traditional "feel." Cottage gardens are characteristically very full, giving the impression of a tapestry of flowers that changes continually throughout the seasons. So use plenty of spring bulbs and low herbaceous flowers under shrubs, and cover vertical surfaces with climbers. Don't worry about "correct" spacing of plants—in a cottage garden they are always crammed in close together.

FAMILY GARDEN

Here everything has been kept as simple as possible, for quick and easy maintenance. The plants used are mainly tough, hardwearing shrubs that will withstand the odd flying football without harm and need little or no pruning—certainly nothing complicated. Prickly or poisonous plants have been deliberately excluded. Plenty of evergreens feature in the planting plan to keep the garden interesting all the year round. A secluded seating spot is well protected from the play area by shrubs, to give a more private area where parents can relax or entertain friends.

SHADY SPOTS

Most gardens contain a mixture of sunny and shady areas as well as places that receive direct sun for around half the day. In the shady spots, such as under trees and big shrubs, or in north-facing beds that get no direct sun, it is essential to select plants that are happy in light shade. Sun-loving plants either won't flower or won't flourish. Although most bright-colored flowering plants need a fair amount of sun, shady areas within a mixed garden can be kept colorful in summer using fuchsias, Begonia semperflorens, impatiens (patience plant), and nicotiana (flowering tobacco), which all do well in light shade.

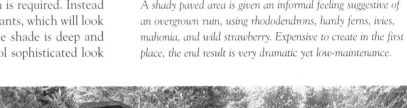

Flowering tobacco is one of the few annual flowers that does well in shade. Use them in groups of to "lift" shady areas or add floral highlights to a sophisticated shady foliage garden. White and green varieties such as this Nicotiana alata "Lime Green" look most at home in these conditions. Plants thrive in borders or, as here, in pots. When grown in strong sun, nicotiana flowers often droop during the day and only recover in the evening, but in a cool shady spot they will remain at their best all the time.

But if a whole garden is in shade, a slightly different approach is required. Instead of trying to create a traditional garden out of shade-tolerant plants, which will look dull, it is much better to create a proper shade garden. If the shade is deep and solid, perhaps created by surrounding buildings, aim for a cool sophisticated look using different kinds of ivies, hardy ferns, euonymus, and ajuga. Look for small nurseries that specialize in these plants in the classified advertisements in gardening magazines; they stock a much bigger range than you find in garden centers.

Find novel ways of using the same plants: ivies, for instance, can be twisted together to make ropes to outline paths or pick out the risers of steps. Add a pretty fountain or formal pool to create sparkle and reflect light into a dark area, and the end result can look stunning even though the range of

A shady paved area is given an informal feeling suggestive of an overgrown ruin, using rhododendrons, hardy ferns, ivies, mahonia, and wild strawberry. Expensive to create in the first place, the end result is very dramatic yet low-maintenance.

ASSESSING TYPES OF SHADE

- ❧ Dappled shade—under a light canopy of trees and shrubs

- ❧ North-facing—no direct sun but reasonable indirect light

- ❧ Deep shade—under large trees or at foot of high walls, often also very dry

- ❧ Damp shade—area surrounded by shrubs, buildings, or fences but where the soil stays moist

KEY PLANTS

- Fuchsias, impatiens, nicotiana, *Begonia semperflorens*

- Ivies, hardy ferns, hosta, Solomon's seal

- "Woodland" flowers (cyclamen, snowdrops, hellebores, and violets)

- Shrubs—(mahonia, berberis, hydrangea, *Euonymus fortunei*, and *Acer palmatum*)

- Acid-lovers—(rhododendrons and camellias)

DESIGN SOLUTION

- Foliage garden

- Woodland garden

- Oriental-style garden

Seating areas don't always have to be in the sun: a shady spot, as shown here, can be a very cool, calm place to relax during the heat of summer. The shady conservatory is a good place to grow houseplants and ferns for the summer. Avoid traditional conservatory plants, which need much more sun.

plants is very limited. Where practical, paint surrounding walls white or add mirrors if the site is very sheltered and not used by children.

If the shade consists of the light, dappled shadow created by trees, a woodland garden makes a good solution which doesn't necessarily look out of place, even on a modern housing development. This style of garden makes a feature of the overhead canopy to grow plants such as rhododendron, Japanese maples, carpets of early spring bulbs, hardy cyclamen, hellebores, violets, and shrubs such as berberis and mahonia.

Add to the woodland theme by making meandering paths surfaced with loose chipped bark and edged with fallen logs. Make a feature of wooden structures such as a mock tree house. You could also use a shady garden to create a Japanese effect, using raked sand, cobblestones, a stone lantern or deer scarer, plus a very few plants such as Japanese maple, ferns, and trimmed euonymus, and even a collection of potted conifers and small trees on tiered shelves. The latter need much less watering in shade than in sun, and so long as the shade is only light, do very well.

Ivies are much more versatile than is generally realized. Twist the stems of climbing or trailing varieties together to make "ropes" which can be used to "underline" steps, or define the edge of a path— or, as here, supported by real rope, to make living garlands perfect for decorating a rather formal graveled area.

HOT SUNNY SITUATIONS

Sunny sites are generally good for plants as long as the soil contains plenty of organic matter to help it retain moisture. Bedding plants and most shrubs will do very well, producing a very colorful garden. The warmth will let you grow a slightly more exotic range of plants than would be possible in less favored spots, so make the most of them.

You could create a gravel garden, in which heat-loving architectural plants of various shapes and sizes are teamed with a background of gravel and paving instead of lawn, which doesn't like hot conditions. Very brightly colored or exotic-looking plants help make this style. Go for a mixture of evergreen herbs and grasses like festuca, some succulent plants such as sedums, spiky-leafed phormiums, and the

A courtyard-style garden makes the most of a hot, sunny spot by providing ideal conditions for slightly tender plants, letting you create a Mediterranean- style garden with a built-in vacation mood. Put the extra wall space to good use: climbing roses thrive, and the warm sheltered air magnifies the scent.

Where the soil is fairly good, a hot, dry, sunny garden gives plenty of scope for growing a wide variety of fascinating plants; go for drought-tolerant species such as phlomis, helianthemum, cistus, cordyline, and herbs to cut down time needed for watering, particularly if the use of hoses is frequently restricted in your area.

cordyline palm. Choose the hot bright colors of phygelius and red hot pokers, climbers like passionflower, and heat-loving annuals such as French marigolds, helichrysum, and verbena. Add a few exotic, subtropical-style flowers like cannas, ginger lily (*Hedychium*), and perhaps a few dahlias (the compact kinds are easier to fit into a mixed planting scheme like this). If the area is enclosed by high walls or fences, it would be perfect for creating a semi-formal courtyard garden. Surface it with gravel or paving; grow slightly tender shrubs and climbers trained on the walls. Ceanothus, passionflower, *Ampelopsis brevipedunculata* "Elegans" and purple grape would all be good choices with perhaps a formal water feature or flower bed with carpet bedding in the middle. Herbs also thrive in the heat and, instead of mixing them with other plants, you might like to create a proper herb garden. This could be formal—round or square, divided by paths into geometric segments for beds, using evergreen and annual herbs, both culinary and old-fashioned medicinal types. You could add other traditional decorative features like a sundial in the center and dwarf lavender or box edging around the beds.

A herb garden can also be more informal, like a series of beds with paths meandering through. Add other appropriate features such as lawns made of chamomile or thyme, which shouldn't be walked on much—use stepping stones if you need to cross them often. Taller plants such as bay can be trained into shapes such as pyramids or standards, or grown in large decorative containers.

Since herb gardens smell so delicious, it is a good idea to add a seat, perhaps under a rose-covered arch or arbor. Scented plants are a must in a warm sunny spot, specially where the air is still and humid. In these conditions, plants impart more of their aromatic oils, which then hang on the air. Place plants with scented leaves near the edge of a path or in cracks between paving where they will be lightly bruised as people pass by, to release the scent. Scented flowers such as old-fashioned nicotiana and lavender are best planted in good-size clumps so their scent will be more noticeable.

Grass does not do very well in a hot, dry spot, so use the opportunity to be creative with paving. Drought-loving plants will thrive in the cracks, so long as slabs have been laid over good soil. Go for alpine pinks, sedums, creeping thymes, feverfew, erigeron, and ajuga for a good year-round paving display. Similar plants can continue the theme up into dry stone walls or containers nearby.

KEY PLANTS

- Bedding plants
- Herbs and scented plants
- Grasses
- Succulent plants
- Phormium, yucca, ceanothus, cordyline
- Phygelius, red hot poker, *Sedum spectabile*, dahlia
- Passionflower, grape vine

DESIGN SOLUTION

- Courtyard garden
- Subtropical beds
- Herb garden

WET CLAY SOIL

This is the soil type that worries gardeners most but, when properly dealt with, it can actually be much better to work with than you expect. The trick lies in digging plenty of grit into the top spade-depth to improve aeration and drainage. Avoid digging too deeply or you risk bringing to the surface the blue or yellow subsoil in which nothing grows. By opening up the texture with grit, clay becomes easier to dig and hoe, and won't set solid or crack in summer. Use clay-with-grit that stays wet all year round to grow waterside plants such as lythrum, houttuynia, Iris laevigata, go-anywhere shrubs like buddleia, Viburnum opulus "Sterile" (the snowball tree), miscanthus and Sambucus nigra cultivars, though not racemosa, which needs better soil.

Roses of all types do very well on moist clay soil, so long as it is not waterlogged, so add lots of organic matter as well as grit. If you want a theme for a garden on clay, use these plants as the bones of a wild or natural-look garden. On improved clay, you can also add plants that are only present in summer, since it is in winter that the worst wet occurs, causing plant roots to rot. Go for annuals which enjoy soil that does not dry out badly in summer. Choose wilder-looking kinds such as linaria for a natural-look wild-flower garden. In a cultivated garden use more conventional annuals plus tuberous plants like dahlia, chocolate-scented cosmos, and gladioli, which are lifted in late fall and stored for the winter as dry tubers in a frost-free shed. As before, to grow any of these well on clay, it is essential to add plenty of well-rotted organic matter and grit.

Plants that need drier roots in winter, like lilies, rosemary, or hebes, never do well, even on improved clay. If you do want to grow them, keep a few in large pots on paved areas. They can also be dotted around the garden in summer or sunk up to their rims in the soil of the borders. In winter, round them up and return them to the paved areas of your garden; in very cold spells wrap the pots or stand them

Town gardens often have heavy clay soil. Here the problem of winter wet has been resolved by creating slightly raised beds filled with good topsoil to provide some drainage. Since grass quickly gets muddy in a small garden on clay soil, the lawn has been completely replaced by paving—a much more practical all-weather surface.

CULTIVATION TIPS

❦ Add lots of grit and organic matter to improve drainage

❦ Grow summer plants (e.g. annuals and dahlias)

❦ Grow damp-hating perennnials in pots

Cultivars of the wild elders (Sambucus nigra) are superb small trees or shrubs for wet clay soil because, of all the ornamental elders, these are the most tolerant of poor conditions. Look for gold-leafed, variegated, or purple-leafed forms—this is "Guincho Purple," one of the best, with dark foliage and large, flat, pale pink clusters of flowers.

KEY PLANTS

❧ *Iris laevigata*, lythrum, astilbe, hosta, houttuynia, mimulus, and roses

❧ Buddleia, *Viburnum opulus, Sambucus nigra*

DESIGN SOLUTION

❧ Raised beds

❧ Container garden

❧ Wild (natural-look) garden

❧ Marsh garden

in a cold greenhouse or porch to stop the roots from freezing solid.

If you have set your heart on growing plants that need good drainage, make raised beds. Retaining walls can be made of brick, reconstituted stone or dry stone, filled in with a mixture of your own topsoil plus grit and well-rotted organic matter such as compost. A garden of raised beds is quite expensive to build, but is very easy to maintain as you can work sitting on the edge of the beds—ideal for older people. An area of raised beds with paving or gravel paths around them makes a great patio garden for people who like to entertain outdoors, since there is plenty of sitting space. You can even extend the walls of the beds to form seats that can then be topped with cushions. It is also a good way of growing small choice flowers like rock plants, as they are up close where you can see them easily and are less likely to be smothered by weeds.

Dahlias do well on improved clay soils, since their tuberous roots are dug up in winter (when clay is wet and sticky) and stored in trays in the shed. Annuals such as the lavatera and rudbeckia here are also "safe" since they are only present in summer. Any other plants that remain all year round, however, should be tolerant of winter wet, like rodgersia.

DRY SANDY SOIL

Although a hot, sunny site offers lots of exciting possibilities, problems will arise where the soil is dry, sandy, or stony because, besides drying out badly, it is also lacking in nutrients and organic matter. Here, improving the soil helps, but compost disappears from this soil within weeks and fertilizer washes straight through it. This garden will always look thirsty, unless you choose the right kinds of plants from the beginning.

Californian poppies thrive in hot dry conditions, though like most plants they need care to get them established in the first place. The easiest method is to sow seed where you want the plants to flower, keeping them well-watered in the early stages. Otherwise, sow thinly in small pots and plant out whole pots without disturbing the roots—again keeping them well-watered at first. Plants will self-seed where happy, and spread themselves without help.

Heat- and drought-tolerant plants are the answer. Plants such as verbascum, dianthus, hebe, cistus, evergreen herbs like the ornamental sages, rosemary and creeping thyme, anything with silver foliage like artemisia, and plants with thick succulent leaves like sedum and sempervivum will all enjoy hot, dry, poor soils. A lot of tough "grow-anywhere" trees and shrubs such as broom, birch, and buddleia will also suit these conditions. However, the main problem with this type of soil is getting things established in the first place. Plant in the fall, when winter rain will keep the plants moist, and dig lots of organic matter into the bottom of the holes before planting.

Red valerian is a wildflower with a long flowering season that thrives in hot, dry, sunny situations on poor soil. It seeds itself easily—but without being too invasive—creating a natural look that is specially effective in a dry stone wall, amongst paving, or in a cottage-style garden. Team it with other self-seeding annuals and perennials for a wilder look. The only work involved is pulling out any plants that come up where you don't want them—or perhaps where you have to walk.

A slightly minimalist approach often looks good when conditions are harsh. Accentuate the dry garden look by using lots of stone, gravel and drought-tolerant plants, especially those with stark shapes. Grasses, daisy flowers such as gazania and osteospermum, and spiky leaves like those of juniper all work well.

If you must plant in spring or early summer—for instance, annuals—then almost daily watering will be needed until the plants become established. On the design side, trying to use specialized "drought" plants to make a normal garden doesn't look convincing. Aim for a more architectural style that suits the colors and shapes of these plants. You might consider a scree garden, which combines small heat and drought-loving plants with a gravel surface and decorative rocks. Rock plants, junipers, dwarf bulbs, and compact shrubs like *Genista lydia* do well here.

If you prefer a larger-scale drought garden, create a minimalist landscape with striking shapes of brooms, *Euphorbia wulfenii,* and caragana, plus the plants listed earlier. For perennials, choose penstemons, *Verbascum bombyciferum,* and *Sedum spectabile.* Annuals can be tricky, so go for heat-loving kinds like mesembryanthemum, pelargonium, osteospermum, gazania, and portulaca. These are all happy in poor soil. However, even they will need frequent watering until they become established and will need replacing annually as they are not hardy. A less labor-intensive alternative is to choose hardy annuals that enjoy the conditions, and leave them to self-seed. Plant the first batch of plants, then don't pull them out in the fall until after they have shed their seed. As they have not been transplanted, the self-sown seedlings develop a much stronger root system and can look after themselves. Go for nasturtiums, *Eschscholzia californica* (Californian poppy), alyssum, valerian, and wallflowers. Self-sown seedlings drift slowly round the garden making an attractive, natural look, coming up in cracks between paving or in gravel paths—ideal for a cottage or similarly informal garden.

Because of all "problem" soils, this is the type that lawns like least, gravel or paving is the best surface covering. By way of a bonus, water droplets condense underneath it at night, and plants deliberately grow their roots under stones in dry soils to find water. So don't fight the conditions—instead, go with them.

KEY PLANTS

- Verbascum, dianthus, cistus, hebe, *Euphorbia wulfenii*

- Evergreen herbs

- Silver foliage plants

- Broom, gorse, genista, birch, buddleia, juniper, rock plants

DESIGN SOLUTION

- Rock garden

- Mediterranean garden

- Stone (gravel) garden

Since grass does not enjoy dry, sandy conditions, it is perfectly feasible to create a "walk-through" garden entirely covered by drought-resistant plants, decorated with rocks and occasional paving slabs strategically placed as "stepping stones." A surface dressing of stone chippings helps to retain moisture in the soil besides making an attractive "mulch." Good plants to include, as shown here, are thrift (Armeria maritima), phormium, cistus, and arctotis.

ACID SOIL

It is possible to get a hint that soil is acid just by looking at what grows there naturally. In areas of heathland, soil is often acid and sandy. Woodland very often has rich, acid soils due to the amount of leaf mold that builds up. But even some clay soils can be acidic. You can get a clue if your neighbors can grow rhododendrons, or by asking local nurseries or garden clubs. But the only way to be sure is to do a soil test with the kit supplied with this pack.

When you know the soil is acid, rule out plants that prefer these chalky soils—like pinks, gypsophila, and scabious. If it is strongly acid, stick to acid-lovers only. However, a lot of mainstream garden plants will grow on any reasonable soil regardless of whether it is slightly chalky or slightly acid, so you can create any normal kind of garden with the added bonus of plants like camellias that need acid soil. If you decide to make the most of the opportunity to create an acid garden, this will usually be based on shrubs since it is in this group of plants that most of the true acid-lovers are found.

Acid-loving plants naturally tend to look good together, so it is easy to create attractive plant associations. Birch, rhododendrons, pieris, and gaultheria make a good all-year-round plant association. Small woodland plants also enjoy acid conditions so long as the soil is rich in organic matter and they have light dappled shade—birch and Japanese maple both create a light canopy under which shade-lovers thrive.

But since many of the better-known acid-loving shrubs, such as camellias, flower in late spring and early summer, it is worth looking out for plants that have something to offer at other times of year, such as Japanese maples and witch hazel.

Camellia flowers are among the most beautiful in the garden. Hundreds of different named varieties are available in shades of pink, red, or white with flower shapes varying from the traditional (above) to waterlily- or anemone-centered kinds. Plants need acid soil that stays moist but not waterlogged, and sun or light shade.

Camellias are normally treated as freestanding shrubs, but can look especially striking when trained against a wall or, as here, framing a gateway. In a cold area this is beneficial, because the flowers are likely to remain in good condition longer given the shelter of the wall.

KEY PLANTS

- Rhododendron, camellia, pieris, gaultheria, vaccinium

- Japanese maple, witch hazel, pernettya, skimmia

- Heaths

- Conifers, birch, tree heath

DESIGN SOLUTION

- Woodland garden

- Heath and conifer garden

This country garden look is achieved using a border of various rhododendrons (including the deciduous kinds previously known as azaleas) against a background of tree and shrub foliage. Spring is the most colorful season in a garden like this, though early-flowering bulbs, the foliage of acers and eucalyptus, as well as herbaceous flowers provide interest during other seasons.

Hydrangeas will grow anywhere, given moist soil, and are specially useful for shady areas where good flowering shrubs are hard to find. However, it pays to match the variety with your soil conditions, so look at the label when buying. As a general rule blue varieties stay blue best on acid soil while pink varieties keep their color best on alkaline soil. White varieties and some of the species hydrangeas will grow in any soil.

As well as woodland-type plants, heaths and conifers form another large group of plants suitable for acid soil and they naturally look good together. These need full sun and a rich but well-drained soil, and an acid sandy soil is fine if you add lots of organic matter. By choosing varieties from all the different species of heaths, it is possible to have some plants in flower virtually all the year round. Some heaths have especially striking foliage in foxy-red, orange, or gold. But since a heath and conifer bed tends to look rather the same all year round, add some grasses, a few evergreen shrubs (particularly acid-lovers with berries), and even deciduous shrubs or herbaceous flowers to vary the view. Add birch if you want a tree, tree heath if you want a larger, shrubbier version of a heath to give height to the middle of a bed.

The perfect finish for any kind of acid bed is a bark or wood-chip mulch (this can also be used for other types of soil): a layer an inch deep all over the soil helps to hold moisture and smother annual weeds, as well as setting off plants beautifully. Bark or wood mulches also look good as path surfaces, and stepping stones made from slices of log, which maintain a woodland character, are a good alternative to paths through very informal acid garden areas. (Tack wire netting over to make them non slip in damp weather).

CHALKY SOILS

Chalky soils are not necessarily those that have great lumps of white chalk rock showing. The term can also mean any kind of soil that is alkaline, which can include clay or sandy kinds, while some peaty soils can be chalky. So again, do a soil test or ask advice locally before choosing plants.

Clematis thrive on soil containing some chalk, though they need rich, fertile, moisture-retaining ground to thrive. Improve a poor soil for clematis by digging in lots of well-rotted organic matter, such as garden compost, before planting, then mulch every spring, and feed throughout the growing season with a liquid feed.

Some plants actually prefer chalky conditions. The best-known are dianthus, gypsophila, and scabious, which naturally combine to make a good plant association, as well as clematis. The first three all need good drainage and the last needs rich soil with fair drainage. The only plants you should rule out are those that need acid conditions. Even if you add peat to the soil and feed with one of the sequestered iron products available in garden centers they will not thrive in the long term. However, if you really can't live without a camellia or rhododendron, choose one of the more compact kinds and grow it in a large tub or half barrel filled with ericaceous compost in a shady corner of the terrace.

However, most normal garden plants grow in most reasonable soil, regardless of it being slightly acid or slightly chalky. Roses can be grown in quite heavy soils if you add lots of organic matter, especially horse manure. On a light chalky soil, grow the species roses, which are more tolerant of poor growing conditions.

The worst type of chalky soil is one that has chalk rock close to the surface. These conditions are very alkaline indeed, and also very poor and dry. However, even this can be made into a garden: the secret lies in adding huge amounts (up to four times the usual amount) of organic matter regularly, especially animal manure, leaf mold, or rotted pine needles, since they are the more acidic forms of organic matter. Add them to the planting holes before putting in new plants, and spread as a mulch twice a year over all exposed soil in spring and fall. On dry soil this will disappear fast, but the soil will gradually improve over time.

If your chalk soil is rocky and dries out badly, avoid both acid-loving plants as well as those that need a moist soil. Go for things that thrive in extreme drainage and poor soil, like the plants suggested in the section on dry sandy soils—it will be far easier to make a good garden. The type of planting schemes suggested there will suit a poor dry chalky soil, too. As a last resort, you might also consider adding a couple of handfuls of the water-retaining gel crystals sold for use in hanging baskets. These remain permanently in the soil and swell up to hold moisture which would otherwise run through fast after rain, thus making it available to plants over a longer time. Though initially expensive, this treatment can make it much easier to get new plants established on what is probably the least hospitable soil it is possible to have in any garden.

Chalky soils overlying chalk rock can be very fast-drying due to the excessive drainage. Don't fight it. Instead, take advantage of the conditions to create a rock garden, using chalk-loving plants such as alpine pinks, gypsophila, and scabious—three plants that particularly enjoy these conditions. Many other drought-tolerant plants will also thrive, such as helianthemum, brooms, and genista.

Chalky borders can support a good range of plants provided the soil contains plenty of organic matter. This one, photographed in the fall, is still full of color thanks to the dahlia "Bishop of Llandaff" Sedum spectabile, *hardy fuchsia, penstemon, and eryngium.*

KEY PLANTS

- ❧ Dianthus, gypsophila, scabious

- ❧ Clematis

- ❧ Cotinus

- ❧ Prunus and malus

- ❧ Verbascum, hardy cranesbills

DESIGN SOLUTION

- ❧ Drought garden

All kinds of pinks thrive on well-drained, chalky soil, and they actually prefer soil without much organic matter. Wild pinks like the Cheddar pink (Dianthus gratianopolitanus) shown here are the least demanding. This can be grown from seed and looks especially good growing in a dry stone wall, or in cracks between paving stones. Cultivated pinks are relatively short-lived and need replacing every three or four years—grow new plants from cuttings taken in mid summer.

Most trees will grow on slightly chalky, alkaline soils, but those with pit fruits, such as cherries and plums (the Prunus family,) are particularly happy. Many ornamental flowering varieties are available, especially of cherries. Check before buying as some become too big for small gardens and, where possible, choose varieties with another asset, such as attractive bark, architectural shape, or fall foliage tints, as the flowering season tends to be short.

SLOPING SITES

A slope can form the basis of a very imaginative and interesting garden. The slope can be treated in several ways. First, it can be made into a series of terraces, each shored up by retaining walls and linked by steps— a good way to make the most of a small site. As the garden is on several levels, conditions such as soil drainage and exposure to sun or wind will vary with each, so that plants needing different conditions can easily be accommodated. You can also fit in many more plants since the different levels allow more air space round them, like having tiered staging in a conservatory. This is a good layout for a plant-lover's garden, but can be expensive if you cannot carry out the work yourself.

Alternatively, you could cut into the slope to create a raised bed on one side, and level the remaining area to lay as lawn or paving. This can make a nicely sheltered, private, low-maintenance garden. A long, shallow slope can simply be left as a slope. A south-facing slope will have a warm sunny aspect suitable for plants such as grape vines and other sun- and warmth-lovers, while a north-facing slope will be cool and shady. Again, both aspects are ideal for different types of plants and planting schemes.

Sloping gardens are usually very dry as water runs off fast, but it makes a good natural site for rock plants and other drought-resistant types, particularly when the slope faces south. Instead of trying to "force" a conventional garden onto such a difficult site, use it as the basis for an attractive natural-look garden, without any beds or borders. Simply plant the whole area with a carpet of plants and level enough space to make narrow paths, which can be paved or graveled, to provide space to walk through. Plants used here included lychnis, anthemis, acanthus, nepeta, stachys, and hardy cranesbills.

Houttuynia cordata "Chameleon" is a moisture-loving plant with ivy-shaped, three-colored leaves and masses of underground runners— useful for helping to stabilize a damp bank. The plant will die down in winter and the new shoots emerge very late in the season, so do not think it has died—it will reappear in mid summer. It is also a good plant for growing in containers.

KEY PLANTS

🌿 Cornus, salix, hydrangea, periwinkle, and ivies to stabilize slopes

🌿 South-facing slopes—heat- and drought-tolerant plants

🌿 North-facing slopes—shade-lovers

DESIGN SOLUTION

🌿 Terraced garden

🌿 Island beds

🌿 Natural-look garden

In a sloping garden, island beds look particularly good cut into natural hollows to accentuate the contours of the garden. This forms the basis of an attractive natural look, in which wild plants are mixed with cultivated ones. You can add to the overall impression by adding rustic seats, arches, and similar features. Island beds are an especially practical way of growing herbaceous plants, since they are accessible for weeding from all sides, while plants grow sturdier and so need less staking than when grown in traditional beds backed by a hedge or wall.

However, a slope can create problems. The soil can be dry as rain runs away fast without soaking in. A slope is also prone to soil erosion when fast-moving water carries the soil away and creates gullies. It is a good idea to sink low walls or railroad ties across slopes as decorative features that will also help to stabilize the soil. This is often done on sloping gravel paths, for instance, where semi-sunken ties are inclined against the angle of slope, forming low steps to stop the gravel working its way downhill. Small areas of steep slope such as banks can be difficult and dangerous to mow if grassed over. They are best planted with low, drought-tolerant shrubs that can be kept tidy by pruning or strimming and have roots which help to bind the soil. Shrubs that spread naturally, such as hypericum, or root as they run, like periwinkle, are most effective at stabilizing banks.

Daffodils or other spring bulbs can be added for seasonal color, since they enjoy well-drained conditions in their summer dormant period. The banks of streams are best stabilized with dogwoods, hydrangeas, or shrubby willows—*Salix alba* cultivars—with roots that withstand winter wet. On a smaller scale, houttuynia works quite well—or, if space allows, plant a few of each to make a decorative and practical streamside scheme.

Rose of Sharon (Hypericum calycinum) *is a useful, tough shrub for covering a bank or stabilizing a sloping garden. It prefers well-drained soil and a sunny situation, but is quite easy-going. Plants are cheap to buy, but also easily raised from cuttings, so it is a useful plant to use in quantity in large landscaping schemes. Trim back after flowering to tidy.*

WINDY EXPOSED SITES

The first task is to establish a windbreak: without it, the range of plants that will flourish is very limited. Most garden plants and shrubs, planted in an exposed site, will grow stunted and the flowers will not last long. White flowers particularly are likely to turn brown in the wind.

Plants with long narrow leaves, especially if they are also very tough and leathery, are often fitted by nature to withstand windy conditions. Pampas grass, bamboos, and miscanthus are all good examples: this is Miscanthus sinensis *"Yakushima Dwarf," a type of ornamental sugar cane. Any of these make good shelter belts round an exposed garden, but are also useful for growing within it along with shrubs.*

Solid windbreaks like walls or fences are not suitable for this situation as they create such a rigid barrier that wind rises over the top and creates eddies inside the garden that can be worse than the original winds. In any case, fences tend to blow away too easily.

What works best is a barrier that sifts out about half the wind, for example small mesh wire or plastic netting, or a tall screen of woody plants. Netting is not pretty, and is best used as a temporary windbreak while a shelter belt of tough trees and shrubs becomes established. After the first winter or two, the plants should be growing well enough for the fencing to be taken down. It could also be left to become incorporated into the framework of the plants to make a denser barrier and keep animals out—when the plants have grown over, it won't be noticed.

Suitable trees and shrubs for this outer defensive layer include *Elaeagnus ebbingei, Rosa rugosa,* miscanthus, holly, elder, and hawthorn, such as the ornamental cultivars of *Sambucus nigra,* not racemosa. In coastal situations, tamarisk, escallonia, and black pine are best able to withstand salt winds. Plant a hedge of all the same species (good in a formal garden), a natural-looking mixed hedge through which some plants are allowed to grow up into small trees (suitable for a country or cottage-style garden), or simply a mixed shrubby border around the boundary of the garden (good for the more casual or family type of garden). When the windbreak has started to grow up and give some protection, more delicate plants can be grown quite happily in the sheltered center of the garden.

Even in a garden well surrounded with trees and shrubs, it is still possible to leave small peepholes through a hedge or border and use them to frame a nice view over the countryside beyond and stop the garden feeling too claustrophobic.

If an enclosed garden is not practical, then you can make a reasonably "normal" garden using only the tougher shrubs and

In trying to shelter an exposed garden with surrounding shrubs, it's easy to end up with a rather closed-in feeling. Counteract this by cutting "peepholes" through hedges or using occasional low-growing plants to break up an otherwise continuous, wind-resistant border round the edge of a garden. Where possible, use these to open out a beautiful view or, in a large garden divided up by internal hedges, use them to give a sneak preview of the next part of the garden.

KEY PLANTS

- *Rosa rugosa*
- *Sambucus nigra* cultivars
- Holly, hawthorn, birch
- Miscanthus

DESIGN SOLUTION

- Wild garden
- Cottage garden
- Country-style garden
- Stone garden

PRACTICAL SOLUTION

- Windbreaks
- Shelter belts
- Tall, tough borders

Seaside gardens are the ultimate windy sites, but even inland gardens without the shelter of nearby trees or buildings can be very exposed. The trick in such situations is to create as much shelter as possible round the edge of the garden. A surrounding wall as shown here works in a very tiny garden especially when used to shelter low-growing plants, but in larger spaces a solid barrier simply causes the wind to eddy— a shelter belt of wind-resistant plants that will filter the wind is a better solution in that case.

low-growing flowers that escape the worst of the wind. Rock plants are particularly suitable, especially those with tough, waxy, or felted leaves, as they are naturally adapted to windy conditions, but drainage must be good.

Alternatively, since the range of reliably windproof plants is rather limited, go for a very minimalist style such as a stone garden. Here, the garden is made entirely from different stone surfaces; various grades of gravel and sand, with cobblestones and a few outcrops of striking chunky rocks grouped together with small associations of suitably wind-resistant plants such as birch or black pine and spreading juniper. The result is striking, very low in maintenance, and looks architectural all year round. It makes a good easy-care front garden for a modern house.

FAMILY GARDEN

A family garden is a compromise. It has to be a "bit of everything." For children and dogs, it should provide wide open spaces for them to run around and perhaps accommodate an outdoor play area. Meanwhile, for adults, it should look good, provide somewhere to sit in the sun, a barbecue, possibly space for a few edible crops, and yet, due to the many other activities that take up a family's time, it must be quick and easy to look after. More detailed advice on low-maintenance gardens appears overleaf.

The garden should also be adaptable to changing needs. As children get older and find outside interests or leave home, the plan should allow for gradual conversion to a more decorative scheme to suit the parents when they have more time to devote to gardening as a hobby.

One of the main requirements in a family garden is plenty of open space for children and dogs to play, where they can't do any harm or get into trouble. A rough, hard-wearing lawn of ornamental ryegrass, together with borders of indestructible shrubs, plus perhaps an old apple tree to swing on, are what are needed. A more ornamental garden for the adults, and other features such as a barbecue area and vegetable plot, are best kept protected from the main play area by substantial plantings of shrub borders or hedges.

Even where space is limited, it is a good idea to divide the garden to provide a separate children's play area (as here, surfaced with soft, springy bark chippings for safety) and a more formal garden for adults. When the family grows up, it is then relatively simple to redevelop the play garden into a new feature for adults. Meanwhile the garden supplies something for everyone.

However, in the early days, a garden suitable for children and pets is best kept as simple as possible. A lawn of hard-wearing grass in the middle, with large evergreen shrubs around the boundaries, is ideal. These should be soft rather than prickly, but choose variegated and flowering kinds as well as plain green to provide color and interest over a long season. Avoid conifers, which tend to be rather prickly, or anything with berries and any plants known to be poisonous, such as laburnum. These are clearly marked in most garden centers now but, even so, it is always advisable to teach children never to put things from the garden into their mouths.

A play area with swings or climbing equipment can be hidden away at the back of the garden behind a tall evergreen screen. The best surface is finely chipped bark, which is much softer than gravel and won't wear out patchily as grass would. It can easily be raked level when scuffed up, lasts for years, and can also be recycled later as surface mulch for beds and borders when the play area is disbanded.

Ponds are best avoided while children are small. A water feature such as a fountain or water gushing up between cobblestones is much safer than standing water, even if it is only shallow. An existing pond can simply be filled in with soil and planted with moisture-loving plants to create a bog garden until the children are older, then excavated again for use as a pond. As a general rule "adult" features like seating areas and vegetable plots should be kept close to the house and made as decorative as possible, since children's games are best conducted well away from windows.

A small salad garden can be productive as well as pretty, using short rows of herbs, red and frilly lettuces, and other salad greens, plus purple-podded dwarf French beans, or yellow zucchini. If you have a barbecue area, the dried stems of vines or aromatic herbs can be burned on the charcoal to add flavor and aroma to the food. Fruit trees and bushes can be grown in the border in place of some ornamental shrubs, or cordon-trained against a sunny wall or fence.

KEY FEATURES

- Tough evergreens
- Robust non-prickly shrubs
- Non-poisonous plants
- Hard-wearing grass
- Play area surfaced with bark chippings
- Barbecue area

DESIGN SOLUTION

- All-year-round garden
- Low-maintenance garden
- Simple design suitable for recycling later

Buddleia davidii is one of the tough, reliable plants that will withstand the rough and tumble of life in a family garden. Buddleia has large pyramidal-shaped flowers in shades of purple, lilac, red and white from mid to late summer which attract butterflies. The plant itself is vigorous and fast-growing so damaged branches are soon replaced, and the shrub is in any case best pruned hard each spring to keep it neat and bushy. If left unpruned, it becomes lanky and the flowers, which develop at the tips of the branches, are soon up out of sight.

SECURITY

Any style of garden can be adapted to provide greater security without looking like Alcatraz. Simple precautions such as gates across the top of the driveway will deter unwanted visitors, while side gates with locks and bolts between front and back gardens make it harder for anyone to get around to the back of the house.

A good, dense hedge is relatively intruder-proof, but when it is also prickly the result is quite impenetrable. The owner of this garden is clearly a believer in providing "belt and braces;" the hedge of Berberis thunbergii "Atropurpurea" is reinforced with a second line of defense—a parallel row of pyracantha— inside which is a rose border.

Prickly plants like roses, berberis, pyracantha, and hawthorn grown as hedges or in borders discourage intruders: even a good dense shrubbery can be pretty impenetrable. Spiky or prickly plants and those that smell strong and unpleasant when damaged, such as *clerodendrum* and lemon balm, also tend to deter vandals from damaging plants or picking the flowers.

Gravel paths and driveways provide some audible warning of visitors. Infrared lights, which come on automatically when anyone comes into the garden after dark, are a useful security measure and double as night lighting if you want to continue a summer barbecue late into the evening, or simply sit and enjoy a floodlit view of your garden. Keep potentially portable items like containers, hanging baskets, or garden ornaments in the back garden where they are not so readily removed.

It is also a good idea to design a front garden (and the back if accessible) so that the middle is fairly open, with low shrubs or flower beds rather than man-high groups. This way, anyone in the garden can be readily seen from the house and by passers-by from the road. Capitalize on this by joining a neighborhood watch scheme.

If newly planted shrubs and trees are at risk of being pulled up by vandals, they can often be secured by pushing several strong hoops of thick wire through the rootball and into the ground at the time of planting. This won't stop determined vandals from breaking them, but by growing varieties that will sprout again from low down, like hypericum, cornus, hydrangea, shrubby willows such as *Salix alba*, amelanchier, and *Acer negundo* "Flamingo," at least the plant will survive. Among smaller plants, the best are those with a good grip on the ground and either don't break or break but leave a stump that will re-shoot. Try ajuga, lemon balm, hardy cranesbills, and *Euphorbia robbiae*. Avoid grafted plants such as roses and clematis, as if the top is broken off, only the rootstock may be left and this will grow into a very inferior plant.

Upright conifers tend to be ruined if the top of the plant is damaged as they always grow out of shape from then on, but spreading conifers like *Juniperus media* cultivars are less likely to suffer badly—and junipers in any case are prickly, and so less attractive to vandals.

If planting a tree, choose one with a tall trunk, with the lowest branches starting at about 7 feet above the ground, so that it is impossible to swing on and break them. Keep choicer plants and those more easily damaged to the back garden where they will be safer, and concentrate intruder-proof plants around boundaries, specially in the front garden, while retaining your main planting scheme.

A high wall is a good deterrent but, for added security, design the garden with a center of low plants so there are no hiding places—this way it's easy to see anyone in the garden. Security lights tend to be more effective in this style of garden too—point the infra-red beam toward gateways or arches where people are most likely to come through. Choose the sort that can be switched on manually, and they double as garden floodlighting for those occasions when you want to sit out and enjoy warm evenings outdoors.

KEY PLANTS

🐾 Roses, pyracantha, holly, hawthorn, berberis, mahonia

DESIGN SOLUTION

🐾 High walls

🐾 Open-centered design

🐾 Security lighting

🐾 Gates

🐾 Avoid visible containers or ornaments

Hedges do not have to be formal; informal flowering hedges look more like straight shrubby borders and are pruned after flowering to tidy them rather than being clipped like beech, box, or yew. Berried hedges can look stunning too, and depending on whether they are pruned or not, can be formal or informal in style. Try growing several varieties of pyracantha together, as shown here, for an interesting and very informal effect; this makes a natural-looking yet impenetrable thicket which keeps livestock, intruders, and pets on the right side of the barrier.

LOW-MAINTENANCE GARDEN

The workload in any garden can be reduced by using residual weedkillers under shrubs and path weedkillers on gravel paths and cracks between paving. Mulch is the non-chemical alternative for use on beds and borders. This involves spreading a 2-inch layer of organic material such as rotted compost or bark chippings over exposed soil each spring to smother developing weed seedlings and so reduce weeding. To eliminate weeds completely, when making a new bed, cover the prepared soil with a sheet of black slitted polyethylene, plant shrubs in the slits, and then cover the plastic with a deep mulch of gravel or large bark nuggets.

It is also possible to choose plants that cut down work. Plants which take most time to look after include annual bedding, any small flowers such as rock plants which are quickly smothered by weeds, edible crops, and containers which need daily watering in summer. Those with the lowest maintenance include ornamental trees,

Paved gardens with raised beds are quick and easy to look after. Use plenty of different surface textures, such as paving and cobbles, to create an interesting effect, even when relatively few plants are used. The raised beds here have been made using old railroad ties—a cheap and attractive alternative to bricks, dry stone, or walling blocks.

Heaths and conifers make a traditionally attractive low-maintenance planting scheme which looks good all year round. Choose a selection of heaths to flower throughout the year, and conifers with a wide variety of shapes and foliage colors. Add a few trees or columnar conifers for height, and use tree heaths in a smaller garden. Birches associate especially well with this plant combination; otherwise choose pines.

KEY PLANTS

🌿 Trees

🌿 Evergreens

🌿 No-prune shrubs and climbers

🌿 Conifers and heaths

🌿 Ground-cover plants

KEY FEATURES

🌿 Permanent mulches

🌿 Drip irrigation

🌿 Simple, no-fuss design

A paved area can be a feature within a large garden, or an entire small garden. It requires very little work to look after—plants are mainly growing up walls or in pots. Here, trimmed box trees of various sizes in pots have been grouped to make an architectural feature in a garden comprised mainly of foliage plants, that need virtually no maintenance apart from a little watering.

evergreens, conifers, and deciduous shrubs. Of these, shrubs are the most time-consuming, especially if you choose buddleia, roses, or other varieties that require annual pruning.

Other garden features take some upkeep too. Lawns need cutting weekly in summer and monthly in winter—paving or gravel is much less work, though more expensive in the first place. Ponds need only slightly less work than a flower bed; excess growth of water weed needs thinning during the summer, while pondside plants and waterlilies need lifting and dividing in spring every few years or they become overgrown.

Garden boundaries should be chosen with maintenance as well as appearance in mind. Fences provide instant shelter and privacy, but have a limited life and need treating with wood preservative annually. If used to support climbers, these must be fixed so they can be lifted down during maintenance. Walls are the most expensive boundaries, but are virtually maintenance-free and provide the best support for permanent climbers.

Hedges are cheapest, take longest to start doing the job, but need cutting. Informal flowering hedges and semi-formal mixed hedges need no more than a light prune to tidy them after flowering. Formal clipped hedges need the most work. If low-maintenance is a priority, choose a slow-growing hedge such as yew or box that only needs clipping once or twice a year, and not privet or *Lonicera nitida*, which will need cutting every four weeks all summer.

The most convenient styles of low-maintenance gardens are small paved or graveled gardens, such as a courtyard or patio garden, a Japanese-style garden, or a stone garden. Evergreens, being the least work of any plants, should form at least two-thirds of the plants used in such a scheme, with a few deciduous shrubs and flowers to add seasonal highlights. If a more conventional design is required, a small lawn or paved area surrounded by borders consisting mainly of evergreen shrubs growing through gravel or heavy-duty bark mulch could form the basis for all types of garden, from family to formal.

YEAR-ROUND INTEREST

It is not difficult to have a garden that looks good in summer, since that is when most of the annual and herbaceous flowers are in bloom. In spring, the job is taken over by blossom and spring bulbs. But in the fall and winter it is very much harder to keep a garden—especially a small one—colorful and inviting. Year-round interest needs planning right from the start. Unfortunately this necessarily means leaving out some of the annual and herbaceous plants that make the traditional blaze of color in spring and summer—after all there just isn't room for everything.

Where there is room to grow a good mixture of plants, use conifers, trees, and large grasses such as miscanthus to create a year-round backbone to the garden. These look spectacular when highlighted with frost in winter, while there are the colors of new growth to enjoy in spring, grass flowers in summer, seedheads and foliage tints to look forward to in the fall, and they create a good backdrop to seasonal flowers.

Instead, evergreens should form the the backbone of the year-round garden. As a good basic rule, allow two evergreens—including conifers, bushy shrubs, and ground covers like heaths—to every other kind of plant. To make a garden which is predominately evergreen look attractive, it is important that each plant stands out from the crowd, instead of just merging into it. So choose plants that provide the greatest possible contrast with their neighbors in shape, size, texture, and color. Look for feathery foliage and large glossy leaves, lime greens and glaucous blue-greens, dramatic upright shapes, neat domes and pyramids, as well as looser tree and bushy shapes. As far as possible, choose evergreens that also provide some seasonal interest, such as flowers or berries. Architectural shapes are particularly valuable. Good plants for this effect include *Fatsia japonica* and bamboo, but don't overlook clipped shapes like topiarized box or standard bay trees in pots.

The non-evergreen plants in the garden should be chosen with even more care. This is the part of the garden that will come and go with the changing seasons, so try to pick as many plants with definite seasonal interest as possible. For winter, there are the white trunks of birches or the red stems of dogwood, which show up especially well against a background of blue conifers or dark evergreens. For spring, clumps or carpets of dwarf spring bulbs such as crocus or miniature daffodils will add useful color without taking up much space. These kinds also have short foliage that dies down early without leaving lots of untidy straggly leaves. In summer, a few carefully chosen spire-shaped herbaceous plants are useful for growing up between the evergreens to contrast with the frequent dome and bushy shapes.

Heavenly bamboo (Nandina domestica) is not related to bamboo at all, but is actually a member of the berberis family. Although not often seen, it is a plant with a great deal of potential—a striking, medium-sized evergreen shrub with attractive foliage and good fall color that makes a useful addition to a year-round garden. Grow it alongside bamboo for a faintly oriental look.

Grasses such as miscanthus and "Bowles Golden" are specially useful in a year-round garden, since they add much-needed movement to otherwise rather stiff and unbending evergreens. In the fall, add late flowers such as schizostylis and Japanese anemones, plus some fall color from Japanese maples or nandina. A good tree for a garden like this would be either a small evergreen, perhaps a strikingly shaped conifer like a blue spruce, or a garrya for winter catkins. A weeping birch or Kilmarnock willow would add an interesting shape—a good hiding-place for small children. But my favorite for a real all-year-round garden would be a small deciduous flowering tree which also provided fall foliage tints, such as a Mount Fuji cherry or an amelanchier.

KEY PLANTS

- 🌿 Weeping birch, Mount Fuji cherry, amelanchier
- 🌿 Architectural plants
- 🌿 Evergreen shrubs, conifers, and grasses
- 🌿 Topiary shapes and dwarf box edgings
- 🌿 Shrubs providing several seasonal interests

KEY FEATURES

- 🌿 Architectural features (e.g. sundial or birdbath)

DESIGN SOLUTION

- 🌿 Foliage garden
- 🌿 Formal garden

In winter, gardens take on a totally different character when outlined by frost. Evergreen leaves stand out starkly, and plants with colored bark such as the shaggy red-brown Acer griseum here look more noticeable than ever. Plan for a good "frost" garden by using lots of dramatic architectural shapes. Conifers, evergreens, seedheads, and upright stems of plants like bamboo all add to the effect.

One of the best ever trees for a small garden is Amelanchier lamarckii, with something to offer in every season. In spring it has palest pink blossom offset by bronze-tinged young foliage and in summer the red berries attract birds. The fall color is sensational, and even in winter the umbrella-like shape makes an elegant addition to the garden. It is also very easy to grow and very tolerant of poor conditions.

TREES

Acer negundo "Flamingo"
D 46-by-26-foot, type of box elder known for foliage coloring, developing from light pink in spring to green with white and pink variegations in maturity, hardy, prefers well-drained soil. ○

Amelanchier lamarckii (snowy mespilus)
D 16-by-13-foot, dome-shaped head, spring blossom and fall foliage tints, most soil especially acid. ○◗

Aralia elata (Japanese angelica tree)
D 33-foot, enormous compound, variegated leaves with white edges, summer-flowering, rich well-drained soil, and shelter. ○◗

Betula pendula "Youngii"
(Young's weeping birch)
D 10-by-10-foot, dome-shaped weeping tree, branches trail to ground, gold fall color, most conditions including poor, dry, or wet soil and wind.

Caragana arborescens (Siberian pea tree)
D 16-by-16½-foot, upright shape, yellow pea flowers mid spring, most conditions including poor soil, cold and windy, very hardy. Alternative: the weeping form is less common but prettier. ○◗

Crataegus laevigata "Paul's Scarlet"
(double hawthorn)
D 16-by-13-foot, spreading dome-headed tree, double scarlet flowers mid spring, most conditions including poor soil, wet, dry, cold, and windy. ○◗

Gleditsia triacanthos "Sunburst"
D 16-by-10-foot, broad-headed tree, bright yellow acacia-like new foliage turns greener in summer, well-drained soil. Alternative: variety "Ruby Lace" has purple-pewter foliage. ○◗

Laburnum "Vossii" (golden chain tree)
D 13-by-10-foot, bright green bark, cloverleaf foliage, long, pendulous yellow flower clusters, well-drained soil, extra water during dry spells. ●

Malus x gloriosa "Golden Hornet"
(crab apple)
D 16-by-8-foot, upright shape, spring blossom and golden fruit late summer to early winter, most reasonably well-drained soil. Alternative: "John Downie" a more spreading tree but larger flask-

shaped salmon-red fruit, the best for making crab apple jelly. ○

Paeonia suffruticosa (tree peony)
D 3¼-by-5-foot, woody shrub, huge blooms in many colors, rich, organic soil, good air circulation. ○◗

Prunus incisa (Mount Fuji cherry)
D 13-by-10-foot, dense bushy shape, spring blossom on bare twigs and fall color, most reasonably well-drained soil. ○

Pyrus salicifolia "Pendula"
(silver frost weeping pear)
D 23-by-13-foot, weeping branches, silvery foliage, white flowers open simultaneously with young leaves, pear-shaped fruits, well-drained soil. ○

Rhus typhina (stag's horn sumach)
D 6½-by-6½-foot, open branching shape, striking foliage and fall color, most soil including poor and

dry, tends to sucker. Alternative: *R. laciniata* has pretty, finely cut foliage. ○

Rose "Canary Bird" standard-trained
SE 8-by-8-foot, open bushy-shaped species rose, single yellow flowers in late spring (the first popular rose to bloom), most soil though prefers heavier kind. Alternatives: "Ballerina" and "Nozomi" often trained this way and make much smaller trees, "Nozomi" makes a weeping tree. ○◗

Salix caprea "Pendula" (Kilmarnock willow)
D 8-by-6½-foot, compact weeping tree, most soils including poor, wet, windy, but not too dry. ○◗

Sorbus aucuparia (mountain ash, rowan)
D 46-by-23-foot, spreading tree with green leaves turning red or yellow in fall, white flowers in spring, red berries in fall, hardy, well-drained soil. ○

TALL SHRUBS AND CLIMBERS

Actinidia kolomikta (kolomikta vine)
D 15–20-foot, twining climber, woody-stemmed, 3–6 inch leaves, have creamy white upper sections, white cup-shaped flowers in summer. Hardy, well-drained soil. ○

Aesculus parviflora (buckeye)
D 10-by-15-foot, spreading, mound-shaped plant, good isolated on lawns or grouped on banks, bronze leaves turn green in summer, white spikes of flowers. Hardy, disease-resistant, well-drained soil. ○

Akebia quinata (five-leaf akebia vine)
SE climbs to 40 feet, prune to desired height, ornamental-looking but sturdy. Leaves composed of five leaflets, purple flowers in mid-May, large purple fruits in late summer. Well-drained soil. ○◐

Buddleia davidii (butterfly bush)
SE 8-by-6½-foot, bushy shrub, summer flowers attract butterflies, most soils. Prune hard in spring. Alternatives: "Nanho Blue" or "Nanho Purple,"both compact varieties about two-thirds normal size. ○

Buddleia davidii "Harlequin"
SE 6½-by-6-foot, bushy shrub, mauve flowers attract butterflies, variegated leaves; most reasonably well-drained soils. Prune hard in spring. ○

Calycanthus floridus (Carolina allspice)
D 2-by-2-foot, bushy shrub, aromatic, oval, dark green leaves, dark burgundy flowers with spreading petals in early summer. Almost any soil, hardy. ○

Camellia—pink
E 6½-by-3¼-foot, dense shrub, spring flowers, reasonably well-drained but moist lime-free soil, sheltered site. ◐●

Cercis canadensis (Eastern redbud)
D 10-foot tall, possibly up to 20-foot after 10 years. Heart-shaped, dark green leaves turning yellow in fall, deep pink, pea-like flowers fade to pale pink in mid-spring before leaves develop. Very hardy, well-drained soil, avoid transplanting. ○

Chaenomeles (flowering quince)—red, pink
D 5-by-5-foot, bushy shrub, spring flowers followed by large ornamental fruit (non poisonous), most soils, can also be trained flat against a wall but then grows to 10 feet. ○◐●

Chionanthus virginicus (fringe tree, grandaddy graybeard)
D 25-by-25-foot, bushy shrub or small tree requires space to develop, large, dark green leaves turn yellow in fall, drooping panicles of white flowers. ◐◑

Choisya ternata "Sundance"
E 3¼-by-3¼-foot, rounded bushy shrub, golden foliage, well-drained sheltered site, foliage may "scorch" in windy or frosty locations. ○◐●

Clematis—large-flowered hybrid lavender-blue, e.g., "General Sikorsky"
D 10-by-13-foot, climber with huge flowers in summer, rich fertile soil, alkaline soil but also grows where slightly acid, plant where roots shaded but top of plant grows into sun, ideal for trellis, arches, arbor poles, and in large pots. Prune in early spring or not at all, according to cultivar. ◑●

Clematis—large-flowered hybrid purple
D 10-by-13-foot, climber with huge flowers in summer, rich fertile soil, alkaline soil but also grows where slightly acid, plant where roots shaded but top of plant grows into sun, ideal for trellis, arches, arbor poles, and in large pots. Prune in early spring or not at all, according to cultivar. ◑●

Clematis—large-flowered hybrid terracotta-pink, e.g., "Hagley Hybrid"
D 10-by-13-foot, climber with huge flowers in summer, rich fertile soil, alkaline soil but also grows where slightly acid, plant where roots shaded but top of plant grows into sun, ideal for trellis, arches, arbor poles, and in large pots. Prune in early spring or not at all, according to cultivar. ◑●

Clematis—large-flowered hybrid white
D 10-by-13-foot, climber with huge flowers in summer, rich fertile soil, alkaline soil but also grows where slightly acid, plant where roots shaded but top of plant grows into sun, ideal for trellis, arches,

VITAL STATISTICS

A Annual flower, only present in summer;
B Biennial; **D** Deciduous; **E** Evergreen;
H Herbaceous; **SE** Semi-evergreen;
○ Sunny position; ◑ Half-sunny position;
● Shady position

arbor poles, and in large pots. Prune in early spring or not at all, according to cultivar. ◑●

Clematis—large-flowered hybrid with stripes, e.g., "Nelly Moser"
D 10-by-13-foot, climber with huge flowers in summer, rich fertile soil, alkaline soil but also grows where slightly acid, plant where roots shaded but top of plant grows into sun, ideal for trellis, arches, arbor poles, and in large pots. Prune in early spring or not at all, according to cultivar. ◑●

Clematis alpina—blue
D 6½-by-10-foot, climber with small nodding flowers in late spring, rich fertile soil but needs a cool situation, e.g., north-facing, thrives in alkaline soil but also grows where slightly acid, ideal for trellis and growing through medium-size shrubs. No need to prune. ◑●

Clematis tangutica
D 16-foot climber with yellow lantern-shaped flowers mid-summer to fall followed by feathery seedheads in late summer/fall, rich fertile ideally alkaline soil, plant where roots shaded but top grows into sun, ideal for growing through other climbers, trees or large shrubs. Pruning optional. ◑●

Clematis viticella—mauve-pink, e.g., "Kermesina"
D 13-by-16-foot, climber flowering mid-summer to early fall, rich fertile soil, enjoys alkaline soil but will also grow where slightly acid, plant where roots are shaded but top of plant grows up into sun, ideal for scrambling up through trees or large shrubs. Pruning optional. ◑●

Climbing rose—pink, red, white, yellow
SE 8-by-16-foot, depending on cultivar, summer flowers scented in some cultivars, rich fertile heavy soil best, fairly sheltered situation, grow on walls, arches, arbors. Prune after flowering is over. ○

Conifer—*Abies koreana*
E 6½-by-5-foot, loose conical conifer, violet-purple cones produced on young trees, most soils. ○◑

Conifer—dwarf pine, e.g., *Pinus mugo* "Mops," *P. strobus* "Nana"

E 3¼-by-2½-foot, dense bushy shape with characteristic long needles, adds character to the garden, most soils including acid. Teams well with heaths and other dwarf conifers. ○

Conifer—pyramidal, colored foliage, e.g., blue spruce and *Picea pungens* cultivars, e.g., "Koster," "Hoto"

E 6½-by-5-foot, pyramidal conifer, silver-blue foliage, most reasonable soils that do not dry out badly. Good alternative Christmas tree grown in a pot and placed outside after the festive season. ○

Cornus alba (dogwood)

D 6-by-6-foot, bushy shrub, red stems conspicuous in winter when leaves have fallen, some cultivars, e.g., "Elegantissima" also have variegated leaves for summer interest, most soils including wet. ○◗

Cortaderia selloana pumila (dwarf pampas grass)

E 5-by-5-foot, grassy tussock with white plumes in summer which dry and remain through winter, good for architectural shape, most soils. ○◐

Corylopsis pauciflora (buttercup winterhazel)

D 4-by-5-foot, bushy, dense, arched shrub, oval, bright green leaves, tubular or bell-shaped flowers in early to mid spring. Excellent in woodland settings, best in well-drained, acid soil, will tolerate alkaline. ◗

Corylus avellana "Contorta"

D 10-by-12-foot, bushy shrub with curious twisted branches, toothed green leaves, yellow catkins on bare branches in late winter. Slow growing, very hardy. ○◑

Cotinus coggyria (smoke bush) purple-leafed kind, e.g., "Royal Purple"

D 10-by-8-foot, bushy shrub, rounded purple foliage and on mature, happy specimens, clouds of wispy pink flowers in early summer; most soils except very wet and heavy. ○

Euphorbia wulfenii

E 5-by-5-foot, bushy perennial, architectural shape plus lime green flowers in early summer, most fairly well-drained soils. ○

Forsythia

D 8-by-6½-foot, open bushy shrub, masses of yellow spring flowers, most soils. Also makes a good flowering hedge. ○◗

Hamamelis (witch hazel)

D 6½-by-6½-foot, shrub, spidery yellow flowers appear on bare stems in early spring, also good fall foliage tints, not very alkaline or wet soils. Shows up best against a dark background, e.g., evergreens or hedge. ◗

Hedera colchica "Sulphur Heart" (formerly "Paddy's Pride")

E 11½-foot climber with large cream/green variegated leaves, architectural plant with year-round foliage effect, most soils, good for shady walls and hiding eyesores. ●

Hedera helix "Goldheart"

E 8-foot climber with small dark green leaves with central gold splash, most soils, good for shady walls and in pots for training around topiary frames. ●

Hibiscus (tree mallow)—blue-flowered, e.g., "Bluebird"

D 6½-by-3¼-foot, bushy shrub, numerous huge single flowers mid to late summer, needs a warm spot with well-drained soil and shelter to do well but spectacular where happy. ○

Hibiscus (tree mallow)—mauve-pink, e.g., "Woodbridge"

D as above

Hydrangea anomala petiolaris (climbing hydrangea)

D 60-by-80-foot, excellent unsupported climber, white flowers in summer, rich green foliage, also effective ground cover. Hardy, moist soil. ○●

Hydrangea arborescens "Annabelle"

D 5-by-5-foot, domed bushy shrub, huge round white heads of flowers summer to late summer, rich moist soil, doesn't matter if slightly acid or alkaline, the easiest species hydrangea to accommodate—others are very big plants. ◗

Hydrangea macrophylla—blue

D 5-by-5-foot, domed bushy shrub, large rounded heads of flower summer that dry out on plant and last into fall, rich moist soil. Mophead varieties open fully; lacecap varieties have flowers round edge of head and what looks like buds that never open in center. Blue hydrangeas need acid soil to retain color; they turn pink on alkaline soil. Often grown in sun. ◗●

Hydrangea macrophylla—pink

D as above, but pink hydrangeas need alkaline soil to keep their color; they turn mauve or blueish on acid soil. Often grown in sun. ◗●

Hydrangea "Preziosa"

D as above, except red flowers, leaves take on bright reddish fall color. Best on lime-free or acid soil. Often grown in sun. ◗●

Hydrangea quercifolia "Snow Queen"

D 7–10-by-7–10-foot, oval, green, leathery leaves emerge in spring, numerous elongated upright panicles of large white blooms, becoming pink in high summer, leaves turn burgundy in fall. Hardy, partial shade, moist soil are ideal conditions, can withstand strong wind, heavy rain and hot sun. ◗○

Ipomoea (morning glory)

A 8-foot climber, large circular flowers in various colors, rich soil, sheltered site, good for trellis, arbors, obelisks in pots, or hanging baskets. ○

Jasmine nudiflorum (winter jasmine)

D 5-by-6½-foot, floppy shrub, best trained against a wall where it makes a weeping bushy shape, yellow flowers appear in winter on bright green leafless stems, any soil in sun or shade including north walls, but not east-facing. Prune after flowering. ○◗

Kalmia latifolia (calico bush)

D 33-by-33-foot, bushy shrub, glossy, dense, green foliage. In early summer clusters of pink flowers open from crimped buds. Prefers well-drained acid soil. ○

Kolkwitzia amabilis (beauty bush)

D 6½-by-6½-foot, arching bushy-shaped shrub, pale pink flowers with yellow throats, any soil. ○

Lathyrus odoratus (sweet pea)

A 8-foot climbers, multicolored pea flowers all summer often scented, good for cutting, moist fertile soil and some shelter, grow on trellis against walls or up tripods in borders. ○

Leycesteria formosa (flowering nutmeg)
D $6\frac{1}{2}$-by-$3\frac{3}{4}$-foot, tall bush, mauve tassel-like bracts containing purple berries dangle from green cane-like stems, any reasonable soil. ○◗

Lonicera (climbing honeysuckle)
D or SE 1-foot climber, scented flowers in red, salmon and pink shades, any moist soil. ○◗

Lonicera sempervirens "Albana crimson" (crimson trumpet honeysuckle)
D or E height to 12-foot, fast-growing, twining vine, oval leaves, tubular scarlet blooms with yellow stamens. Frost-hardy, well-drained soil. ◗

Magnolia stellata (star magnolia)
D 6-by-6-foot, loose dome-shaped bush, lots of white star-shaped flowers in spring, most reasonable and fairly well-drained soils (unlike many magnolias this does not object to slightly alkaline soil), some shelter. ○◗

Miscanthus sinensis "Zebrinus"
D $6\frac{1}{2}$-by-$1\frac{1}{2}$-foot, upright grass, bamboo-like stems and gold/green striped leaves in summer (bare canes remain in winter); any soil including waterlogged and exposed, not invasive but a row makes a good decorative screen or windbreak. ○◗

Parthenocissus tricuspidata "Robusta" (Boston ivy)
D height to 60 feet, perfect tree or wall climber, red-purple fall leaf color, blue berries in winter. Hardy, well-drained soil. ○◗

Passiflora caerulea (passionflower)
D 16-foot climber, 3-inch pale blue sunburst-like flowers all summer often followed by orange egg-shaped fruit (non-poisonous); mild site, good drainage, prune late spring. ○

Philadelphus coronarius (mock orange)
D $6\frac{1}{2}$-by-6-foot, bushy shrub, single orange blossom scented white flowers in early summer (a few double varieties available), any soil and situation including poor and windy. Prune after flowering. ○

Pieris
E $6\frac{1}{2}$-by-5-foot, bushy shape, red poinsettia-like young foliage and strings of white bell-like flowers in spring, acid soil, some shelter and shade from east side. ○◗

Pieris—variegated
E as above

Polygonum aubertii (silverlace, fleece, or Russian vine)
D height to 40 feet, very fast-growing, woody-stemmed twining climber, clings to arbors, walls, masonry of any kind. Heart-shaped leaves, small white or greenish flowers turning pink in summer–fall, pinkish white fruits.

Pyracantha—red/orange
E 8-by-$6\frac{1}{2}$-foot, prickly bushy shrub, long-lasting berries in fall and winter, makes a good hedge, can also be trained flat against walls. Various named varieties available. ○◗

Pyracantha—yellow
E as above

Ribes (fruiting gooseberry bushes)
D $2\frac{1}{2}$-by-$2\frac{1}{2}$-foot, prickly bushes, flowers late spring and edible fruit summer, deep moist fertile soil, sun; grow in borders as shrubs (standard plants are especially attractive) or as cordons to make garden dividers, or on walls. Prune winter. ○

Ribes (fruiting red or black currant bushes)
D $3\frac{1}{4}$-by-$2\frac{1}{2}$-foot, bushes, ornamental flowers late spring and edible crop of berries summer, deep moist fertile soils, sun. Grow in borders like normal shrubs; red currants can be cordon-trained to make a garden divider or against wall or trellis. Prune winter. ○

Rosa rugosa
SE $6\frac{1}{2}$-by-6-foot, very prickly bushy shape, single pink or white flowers summer and huge red hips that attract birds, most soil, sun, very wind-tolerant. Good for hedges and shelter belts in exposed situations. No need to prune. ○

Rose—bush; orange, pink, red, white, or yellow
D or SE $3\frac{1}{4}$-by-$3\frac{1}{4}$-foot, prickly upright-bushy shape, (usually) double cabbage-like flowers from early summer well into fall, some varieties scented, most soils ideally fertile and heavyish, sun. Prune early spring. ○

Rose—old-fashioned
D or SE 6-by-5-foot, prickly loose bushy shape, unusual flowers sometimes striped or "quartered" often highly scented but short flowering season in early summer. No need to prune beyond deadheading. Large number of varieties available. ○

VITAL STATISTICS

A Annual flower, only present in summer;
B Biennial; **D** Deciduous; **E** Evergreen;
H Herbaceous; **SE** Semi-evergreen;
○ Sunny position ◗ Half-sunny position
● Shady position

Rose—standard
D or SE 4-by-$2\frac{1}{2}$-foot, formal trained shape like rounded bush on top of long stem, flowers all summer, prune early spring, a useful way to fit roses into full borders or formal garden. When ground-cover roses, e.g., "Nozomi," trained as standards, creates a wonderful cascading effect. ○

Sambucus racemosa "Plumosa Aurea" (ornamental elder)
D 9-by-8-foot, domed bushy shrub, bright gold feathery cut-leafed foliage all summer, any reasonable soil, some shelter; can be pruned hard in early spring annually to restrict size. ○

Scarlet runner beans
A 8-foot climbers, pretty red or pink flowers plus edible crop of beans in summer, deep fertile moist soil, sun. Dual-purpose ornamental and useful plant for growing on tripods of canes or rustic poles, or on trellis against a wall or shed.

Syringa vulgaris "President Lincoln"
D 7-by-6-foot, shrub with dense panicles of fragrant, tubular flowers which bloom heavily in alternate years. Hardy, needs deep, fertile, well-drained alkaline soil. ○

Viburnum plicatum tomentosum "Shasta" (Japanese snowball tree)
D 10-by-12-foot, bushy, spreading shrub, dark green toothed, veined, oval leaves. Late spring sees abundant, large white flowers covering branches, with bright red fruit in mid summer. Needs deep, fertile, moist soil. ○◗

Wisteria floribunda "Alba"
D 28-foot high in early summer, woody stemmed twining climber, leaves of 11–19 oval leaflets, scented, drooping racemes up to 2-foot long of white flowers in early summer. Well-drained soil. ○

LOW SHRUBS AND FLOWERS

Abelia schumannii
D or SE 6-by-6-foot, domed bushy shape, lilac-pink flowers early summer into fall, most well-drained soils. ○

Abeliophyllum distichum (white forsythia or Korean abelia-leaf)
D 4-by-4-foot, open shrub, oval, dark green leaves, purple buds in fall open in early spring into fragrant white blossoms. Pest- and disease-hardy, moist, slightly acidic soil. ○◗

Acer palmatum "Dissectum"
D 5-by-3¼-foot, bushy shape, plain green ferny foliage, sheltered site, moist but well-drained lime-free soil. ○◗

Acer palmatum "Dissectum Atropurpureum"
D 5-by-3¼-foot, bushy shape, purple-red ferny foliage, sheltered site, moist but well-drained lime-free soil. ○

Achillea (yarrow)
H 30-by-20-inch, flat-topped heads of yellow pink or red flowers summer, most fairly well-drained soils. ○◗

Agapanthus "Headbourne Hybrids"
H 3¼-foot-by-20-inch, round heads of star-like blue flowers on long stems above bulb foliage in late summer, deep fertile soil. ○

Anemone japonica (Japanese anemone)
H 3¼-by-3¼-foot, upright bushy shape, large fragile-looking flat, round, single, or semi-double flowers in late summer and fall, mainly pink or white, most soils except very wet. ○◗

Aquilegia (columbine)
H 30-by-20-inch, bonnet-like flowers in a range of colors early summer, fairly well-drained soil. ◗

Artemesia "Powis Castle"
H 2-by-2-foot, domed bushy shape, filigree silver foliage summer and fall, non-flowering, well-drained soil. Good background for flowering plants. ○

Arundinaria viridistriata
E 4-foot-by-20-inch, upright mini bamboo, lemon and lime striped leaves, most fairly well-drained soils. ◗

Asclepias tuberosa (butterfly flower)
H 2½-by-1½-foot, tuberous, lance-shaped leaves with small, five-horned, orange flowers in mid to late summer, well-drained soil, thrives in drought. ○

Aster amellus—lavender-purple
H 24-by-20-inch, domed bushy shapes covered with single daisy flowers (purple, mauve, pink shades mainly) fall, fertile soil fairly well-drained. ○

Astilbe—pink, red
H 24-by-20-inch, feathery spikes of pink or cream flowers summer, moist fertile soil. ◗

Baptisia pendula
D 3½-by-2½-foot, long, upright panicles of white pea-like flowers, deep, well-drained, neutral to acid soil. ○

Box—conical-trimmed
E 30-by-10-inch, formal clipped shape, most reasonable soils, tolerates windy site; use to decorate flower borders, in formal gardens or in pots. ○◗

Box—peacock
E 20-by-20-inch, formal clipped shape, most reasonable soils, tolerates windy site; use to decorate flower borders, in formal gardens or in pots. ○◗

Box—sphere-trimmed
E 1-by-1-foot, formal clipped shape, most reasonable soils, tolerates windy site; use to decorate flower borders, in formal gardens or in pots. ●

Campanula persicifolia
H 30-by-30-inch, low clump-forming rosette plants with tall spikes of blue, lilac, or white flowers early summer. Fertile moist soil. ○◗

Caryopteris clandonensis (blue spiraea)
D 3¾-by-3¾-foot, domed bushy shape, gray foliage and fluffy blue flowers late summer and early fall, well-drained soil. ○

Ceratostigma willmottianum (hardy plumbago)
D 2-by-2-foot, domed bushy shape, blue flowers mid summer into fall, reddish fall foliage tints, well-drained soil, shelter. Prune hard late spring. ○

Chrysanthemums—hardy ("Yoder" and *indicum*)
H 20-by-12-inch, upright or domed bushy shapes, single or double daisy flowers in large range of colors late summer and fall, moist fertile soil. ○

Cordyline australis (cabbage palm)—purple
H 5-by-2-foot, spiky architectural shape, all year round foliage effect, most fairly well-drained soils, mild area. Grow in pots or borders. ○

Coreopsis "Moonbeam"
H 18-by-18-inch, delicate, yellow, daisy-like flowers bloom throughout summer, ferny foliage. Good in borders, containers or hanging baskets, drought and mildew resistant, fertile, well-drained soil. ○

Cosmos atrosanguineus (chocolate-scented cosmos)
H 20-by-10-inch, floppy upright shape, like a small dahlia with nearly black deep maroon chocolate-scented flowers mid summer into fall, fertile fairly well-drained soil, shelter, very mild area or lift dormant tubers and store as for dahlias. ○

Crocosmia (montbretia)
H 30-by-20-inch, clumps of lance-shaped leaves, bright orange, red or yellow flowers mid to late summer, fertile well-drained soil, shelter. ○

Dahlia—compact
H 30-by-20-inch, upright bushy shape, large colorful flowers late summer and early fall, moist fertile soil. ○

Daphne cneorum (Garland Daphne)
D 9–12-inches, low-growing shrub, 1-inch, glossy, oval leaves, perfumed, deep pink flowers completely cover plant in spring and again in fall in the south. Well-drained soil, mulch to maintain cool root zone. ○

Daphne mezereum
D 3¼-by-2½-foot, upright bushy shape, fragrant purple flowers on bare stems in spring, rich well-drained soil. ○◖

Dianthus "Bath's Pink"
D 10-inch tall, numerous fragrant, pink, star-shaped flowers appear in late spring, blue-green foliage, well-drained, gritty, lime-rich soil. ○

Dicentra spectabilis (bleeding heart)
H 2-by-1½-foot, loose bushy shape, heart-shaped white or red and white flowers early summer, rich well-drained soil. ◖

Dicentra spectabilis "Luxuriant" (bleeding heart)
H 18–20-inches tall, sprays of delicate cherry pink blossoms blooming continually from mid spring to mid fall, ferny blue-green foliage, moist but well-drained soil. ◖

Digitalis purpurea (foxglove)
B 6-foot-by-20-inch, upright spire shape, purple flowers along stems early summer, moist soil. ○ ◖

Dwarf conifer—green conical, e.g., *Picea* "Albertiana Conica"
E 2-by-1-foot, dense cone shape, fertile well-drained soil not drying badly in summer. ○

Dwarf conifer—green flame shape, e.g., *Juniperus communis* "Compressa"
E 2-by-1-foot, upright flame shape, most fairly well-drained soils. Tolerant of soil that dries out in summer and windy conditions. ○

Dwarf conifer—gold-streaked, open-spreading-vase shape, e.g., *Juniperus media* "Gold Sovereign"
E 16-by-3-inch, low spreading dome with dished center, slightly prickly feathery variegated foliage, well-drained soil. ○

Dwarf conifer—*Taxus baccata* "Standishii"
E 3-foot-by-14-inch, upright pillar shape, old gold foliage, fertile well-drained soil. ○

Dwarf conifer—*Thuja occidentalis* "Rheingold"
E 2½-by-2-foot, bushy flame shape, feathery foxy red-gold foliage, fertile well-drained soil. ○

Echinacea "Bright Star" (coneflower)
E 2-foot tall, large, long-lasting daisy-like blooms from mid summer to early fall, attractive to butterflies, any soil, drought-resistant. ○◖

Eryngium (sea holly)
H 24-by-16-inch, upright bushy shape, silver-blue-gray foliage and spiky metallic-look flowers in summer, light well-drained soil. ○

Euonymus alatus "Compactus" (dwarf flame euonymus)
D 6-by-5-foot, dark green leaves turn scarlet in fall, greenish summer flowers, red and purple fruits. Well-drained soil and full sun for best fall color. ○

Euonymus fortunei "Emerald 'n' Gold"
E 3¼-by-3¼-foot, bushy shape, green/gold variegated foliage, most soils. ○◖

Euphorbia amygdaloides "Rubra" (wood spurge)
H 16-by-12-inch, upright, bushy shape, purple foliage, and lime green spring flowers, most fairly well-drained soils. ○◖

Euphorbia dulcis "Chameleon"
H 1-by-1-foot, low spreading bushy shape, purple foliage and spring flower bracts, then some pinky, fall tints, most fairly well-drained soils. ○◖

Euphorbia polychroma (cushion spurge)
H 1-foot tall, mound-shape, yellow flowers in spring, foliage turns red in fall, well-drained soil. ○

Ferns—hardy, deciduous, feathery leaves, e.g., *Adiantum pedatum* and *venustum*
E 1-by-1-foot, bushy shape, moist fertile soil. ◖

VITAL STATISTICS

A Annual flower, only present in summer;
B Biennial; **D** Deciduous; **E** Evergreen;
H Herbaceous; **SE** Semievergreen;
○ Sunny position ◖ Half-sunny position
● Shady position

Ferns—hardy evergreen, e.g., *Asplenium scolopendrium*
E 16-by-16-inch, shuttlecock shape, architectural foliage, moist fertile soil. ◖

Fothergilla gardenii (dwarf fothergilla)
D 2–3-foot tall, leathery, dark green summer foliage turns yellow and red in fall, spikes of honey-scented flowers in early spring. Tolerates wet situations, acid soil, requires sun to achieve fall coloration. ○

Geranium (hardy cranesbill) — larger kinds, e.g., "Johnson's Blue"
H 2-by-2½-foot, loose spreading dome-shaped, blue flowers early to late summer, fairly well-drained soil, good tall ground cover. Good between shrubs. Other large cranesbills may have pink, magenta, or white flowers. ○◖

Geranium phaeum
H 24-by-16-inch, loose upright bushy shape, deep purple almost black flowers, well-drained soil. ◖

Geum
H 20-by-20-inch, domed clumps, yellow orange or red flowers early to late summer, fairly well-drained soil. ○◖

Gypsophila paniculata (baby's-breath)
H 6-by-3¼-foot, light airy shape, foam-like sprays of white flowers and low rosettes of foliage, light well-drained alkaline soil. Good for cutting. ○

Hakonechloa macra "Alboaurea"
H 1-by-2-foot, weeping shape, grassy clumps, lemon-lime striped foliage, moist soil, also good in pots. ○◖

Helianthus annuus (sunflower, multiflowered variety, not giant type)
A 5-foot-by-20-inch, upright stems, large sunflower heads in yellow, orange, and mahogany shades, most soils. ○

Helleborus orientalis
E 20-by-12-inch, low bushy shape, large single flowers pink burgundy or spotted in spring, well-drained but humus-rich soil. ◖

Hemerocallis (day lily)
H 3¼-by-2-foot, clump-forming, large lily-like flowers in orange, red, and yellow shades, most reasonable soils. ○◗

Hemerocallis "Stella d'Oro"
H 2-foot mound of foliage, blooms in spring and fall with numerous yellow bell-shaped flowers, with green-tipped outer petals, most reasonable soils. ○◗

Hosta—glaucous foliage
H 20-by-30-inch, clump-forming cabbage-like shape, large rounded glaucous-blue foliage in summer, moist humus-rich soil. Slugs and snails a problem. Good in containers. ◗

Hosta—variegated foliage
H 12-by-20-inch, clump-forming foliage plants, large oval variegated leaves, moist humus-rich soil, slugs and snails a problem. Good in containers. ◗

Hypericum calycinum (Rose of Sharon)
E 1-by-3¼-foot, large single yellow flowers with long fluffy stamens all summer, any soil except very wet, good for covering problem banks, poor dry or stony soil, can become invasive, prune to ground early spring annually. ○◗

Iris—bearded
H 3¼-by-2½-foot, clump-forming spiky plants, large geometrically shaped flower heads in various colors early summer, rich well-drained soil. Divide every 3–4 years, 4 weeks after flowering. ○

Iris laevigata
H 20-by-12-inch, clump-forming spiky plants, medium-size, geometrically shaped flowers, mainly pink, white, and blue shades, rich moist soil and pond edges. ○

Iris sibirica
H 20-by-12-inch, clump-forming spiky plants,

medium-size, geometrically shaped flowers, mainly blue, white, and pink shades, moist soils. ○◗

Juncus effusus "Spiralis" (corkscrew rush)
E 12-by-20-inch, architectural splaying shape, corkscrew-like stems all year round, moist soil and pond sides. ○◗

Kniphofia (red hot poker)
E 3¼-by-3¼-foot, fountain of foliage with pokers emerging, red or yellow pokers summer (and fall with some cultivars), well-drained soil. ○

Lavender
E 12-by-20-inch, bushy shape, grayish aromatic foliage and scented lavender flowers summer, well-drained soil. Good for cutting. Clip lightly after flowering. ○

Lilies—orange, white, yellow
H 32-by-16-inch, upright spike shape, large trumpet flowers in summer, short flowering season, rich well-drained soil. Many cultivars need lime-free soil. ○◗

Lobelia "Queen Victoria"
H 30-by-20-inch, bushy upright shape, loose spikes of red flower above purple foliage late mid-summer, moist soil. ○

Lupins
H 3¼-by-2-foot, bushy shape, upright spires of flower various colors plus striking foliage, reasonably well-drained, lime-free soil. ○◗

Lythrum salicaria
H 4-foot-by-20-inch, bushy upright shape, spikes of mauve-pink flowers mid to late summer, moist soil and pondside. ○

Mahonia aquifolium
E 20-inch-by-5-foot, bushy spreading shape, blobs of

yellow flowers in spring and bronzy-green prickly evergreen ground-covering foliage, most reasonable soils, including poor, dry, shady soil under trees. ◗

Milium effusum "Aureum"
(Bowles golden grass)
H 12-by-20-inch, upright grass, bright gold foliage is brightest in spring, moist soil. ◗

Nandina domestica "Firepower"
(heavenly bamboo)
E 3¼-by-3¼-foot, upright clump-forming foliage spring and fall, red berries fall and white flowers in spikes summer, well-drained soil. ○

Nepeta "Six Hills Giant"
H 2-by-2-foot, bushy spreading shape, lavender flowers in summer and aromatic gray foliage, light well-drained soil. ○

Nicotiana (tobacco flower)—salmon
A 12-by-8-inch, informally upright, single salmon tobacco flower all summer and into fall, most reasonable soils. ○◗

Ornamental cabbages
A 1-by-1-foot, cabbage-like shape, pink/mauve or cream/green foliage, well-drained soil or containers. Useful fall and winter bedding plant. ○◗

Paeonia (Peony—herbaceous)
H 32-by-32-inch, domed bushy shape, large chalice-shaped pink flowers early summer, rich well-drained soil. Plant no more than 1 inch deep or won't flower. ○

Papaver orientale (oriental poppy)
H 3¼-by-3¼-foot, splaying bushy shape, huge fragile flowers in white, pink, and red shades early summer, rich well-drained soil. ○

Penstemon—pink, violet-blue
H 24-by-16-inch, splaying open shape, spikes of tubular flowers all summer and into fall, rich well-drained soil including those that dry badly in summer, not hardy in coldest regions. ○

Perovskia atriplicifolia (Russian sage)
D 3¼-by-3¼-foot, splaying bushy shape, long grayish stems lined with lilac-purple dots of flowers late summer and early fall, well-drained soil. Cut to ground each spring. ○

Phlox
H 2½-foot-by-20-inch, upright bushy clumps, large flower-heads in mauve, pink, white, and red late summer, rich reasonably well-drained soil. ○◗

Platycodon (balloon flower)
H 20-by-16-inch, bushy, curious inflated flower buds open to large blue star-shaped flowers mid to late summer, reasonably well-drained soil. ◐

Polemonium caeruleum "Brise d'Anjou"
H 16-by-12-inch, upright stems, gold/green striped foliage, violet flowers summer, well-drained soil. ◐

Polygonatum (Solomon's seal)
H 2-by-2-foot, upright clump-forming shape, architectural shape, plus white bell flowers dangling from stems in spring, moist humus-rich soil. ◗

Potentilla fruticosa "Sunset" (buttercup shrub or cinquefoil)
D 1-by-2-foot, compact-growing shrub small, dark green leaves, red or orange yellow blooms. Almost any soil, warmth gives a richer color to flowers. ◐

Primula—candelabra type, e.g., *P. pulverulenta*, *P. japonica*
H 2½-by-1-foot, rosettes of leaves with upright pink, mauve, yellow, orange, or white flower spikes depending on variety, moist humus-rich soil. ◗

Primula denticulata (drumstick primula)
H 8-by-8-inch, rosettes of leaves, lavender or white "drumstick" flowers in spring, humus-rich soil. ◗

Rhododendron yakushimanum hybrids
E 3¼-by-3¼-foot, domed bushy shape, pink tawny and cream flowers early summer, acid soil, shelter. ◗

Rose—patio type (orange, pink, white, or yellow)
SE 20-by-32-inch, spreading bushy shape, medium-size flowers summer to fall, most soils, Good for front of borders and containers if kept well watered. ○

Rosmarinus (rosemary)
E 32-by-24-inch, spreading bushy shape, evergreen foliage and blue flowers early summer, well-drained

soil. Also good for patio pots and culinary use. ○

Rudbeckia (coneflower)
H 32-by-20-inch, upright-bushy shape, large orange daisy flowers with black centers mid summer to fall, perennial, most fairly well-drained soils. ◐

Salcia verticulata "Purple Rain"
H 2-by-1½-foot, long arching spikes of purple buds open throughout summer into a mass of small flowers, sun, fertile, well-drained soil, hardy to frost. ○

Salvia officinalis "Purpurascens" (purple sage)
SE 12-by-20-inch, bushy-clump shape, oval purple foliage, well-drained soil. ◐

Salvia x superba "Blue Hill"
H 16–20-inch, numerous bright blue flower spikes, tubular two-lipped flowers and aromatic foliage, blooms all summer, neat plant for edging or borders, any soil with good drainage, drought-tolerant. ○

Santolina (lavender cotton)
E 12-by-20-inch, bushy shape, aromatic gray foliage plus yellow flowers summer, well-drained soil. ○

Sarcococca hookeriana "Digyna"
E 4-by-4-foot, bushy, fragrant white flowers early spring, most soils. ◐

Scabiosa (scabious)
H 2-by-2 foot, bushy shape, large round flat blue button-like flowers in summer, well-drained alkaline soil, attracts butterflies. ○

Scabiosa columbaria "Butterfly Blue"
H 12-inches tall, dwarf scabiosa, flowers from spring to fall with heaviest blooms in spring, 2-inch flowers attract butterflies, well-drained, light soil. ○

Schizostylis (kaffir lily)
H 12-by-20-inch, upright clump-forming, pink,

VITAL STATISTICS

A Annual flower, only present in summer;
B Biennial; **D** Deciduous; **E** Evergreen;
H Herbaceous; **SE** Semievergreen;
○ Sunny position ◗ Half-sunny position
● Shady position

white, or coppery flower spikes in fall, moist soil. ○

Sedum spectabile (showy sedum)
H 30-by-30-inch, splaying bushy shape, large flat pink flower-heads in fall, well-drained soil, attracts butterflies. ○

Sisyrinchium striatum
H 24-by-12-inch, upright clumps, cream/yellow flowers on iris-like foliage in summer, most soils. ◐

Skimmia japonica "Foremanii"
E 3¼-by-3¼-foot, domed bushy shape, clusters of red berries in winter, acid or lime-free soil, good container plant while young. Needs a male plant for pollination or no berries—plant with "Rubella." ◐

Skimmia japonica "Rubella"
E 3¼-by-3¼-foot, domed shape, large bunches of pink flower buds in winter, acid or lime-free soil. ◐

Spiraea japonica "Anthony Waterer"
D 3¼-by-3¼-foot, open bushy shape, flattish heads of pink flower mid to late summer, most soils. ◐

Spiraea japonica "Gold Flame"
D 3¼-by-3¼-foot, bushy shape, bronze-orange foliage brightest in early summer, most soils, cut to ground every spring. ◐

Spiraea Japonica "Shibori"
D 2–3-by-2–3-foot, weeping branches covered in white, red, and pink blooms, good as edging plant or for limited spaces, fertile well-drained soil. ○

Weigela florida "Foliis Purpureis"
D 32-by-32-inch, bushy shape, deep pink flowers in early summer and purple foliage, most soils. ◐

Weigela florida "Variegata"
D 4-by-4-foot, bushy shape, pale pink flowers early summer, cream/green foliage, most soils. ◐

Yucca filamentosa "Color Guard" (Adam's needle)
E 6-by-5-foot, basal-rosetted shrub. Striped green and cream leaves, white, tulip-shaped flowers in summer. Hardy to frost, well-drained soil. ○

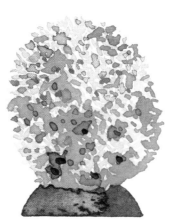

GROUND COVER

Acaena (New Zealand burr)
E 3-by-16-inch, mats of small green or pewter foliage with pretty red or brown burrs late summer, most well-drained soils including poor, dry, and stony, good for cracks in paving. ◐◗

Ajuga (bugle)
H 4-by-18-inch, creeping, purple bronze or tricolored foliage, plus short blue spikes of flower all summer, any soil including poor and wet, can be invasive. ◐◗

Alchemilla (lady's mantle)
H 6-by-6-inch, clumps, elegant pleated fan-like leaves and lime green flowers summer, well-drained soil. ◐◗

Anemone blanda
H 2-by-2-inch, tufts, large daisy flowers in various colors spring, reasonably well-drained humus-rich soil. ◐◗

Asarum europaeum (European ginger)
H 12-by-6-inch, glossy, green, round, or kidney-shaped leaves, tiny brown flowers at ground level, moist soil, good in rockeries or wooded areas. ●

Aubrietia
E 4-by-18-inch, trailing mats, cascades of small mauve, purple, or pink flowers spring, well-drained soil, good for rockeries. ○

Bedding plants—mixed colors
A 12-by-6-inch (varies), upright-clump, planted as carpets for massed color effect, humus-rich well-drained soil. ○

Bergenia
E 12-by-18-inch, clumps, large cabbage-like foliage and pink spikes of flower spring, any soil including poor, wet or dry. ◐◗

Brunnera
D 12-by-18-inch, spreading clumps, airy sprays of forget-me-not-like flowers spring to mid-summer and large kidney-shaped leaves, most soils. ◗

Calluna—flowering
E 8-by-18-inch, clumps, pink, mauve, purple, or white bell flowers mid-summer to fall, acid soil including exposed sites. ○

Calluna—red foliage
E 8-by-18-inch, clumps, feathery red/gold/orange foliage (various cultivars) with pink, mauve, or purple bell flowers mid-summer to fall, acid soil including exposed sites. ○

Campanula—creeping, e.g., *C. carpatica*
H 8-by-18-inch, mats, star-like blue flowers all summer, well-drained alkaline soil. ◐◗

Convallaria majalis (lily of the valley)
H 6-by-12-inch, spreading tufts, highly scented, white bell flowers spring, most soils. Slow to establish. ◗

Cotoneaster—prostrate forms, e.g., *C.* x *suecicus* "Coral Beauty"
E 2-by-5-foot, loose mat, red berries late summer and fall, any soil. ◐◗

Crocus
H 4-by-2-inch, spring flowers mauve, purple, and yellow, reasonably well-drained soil. ◐◗
Daboecia
E 12-by-18-inch, clumps, heath-like plants with large purple or pink bell flowers all summer, acid soil including exposed sites. ○

Dianthus (pinks)
E 10-by-10-inch, pink flowers summer, well-drained alkaline soil. ○

Diascia
H 12-by-18-inch, mask-shaped pink flowers all summer and into fall, well-drained soil. ○

Dwarf box—edging plants, e.g., *Buxus sempervirens* "Suffruticosa"
E 6-by-4-inch, plant in rows and trim to shape, edging for beds, most soils. ◐◗

Dwarf conifer—*Chamaecyparis* "Green Globe"
E 12-by-12-inch, neat bun shape, fertile well-drained soil but not drying out badly in summer. ○

Dwarf conifer—*Chamaecyparis obtusa nana gracilis*
E 12-by-12-inch, bushy shrub, green lacy fans of overlapping foliage, well-drained soil. ○

Dwarf conifer—*Juniperus squamata* "Blue Star"
E 12-by-20-inch, dense, low, hump shape, deep blue winter foliage turns silver-blue in summer, well-drained soil. ○

Dwarf conifer—*Thuja orientalis* "Aurea Nana"
E 28-by-16-inch, dense, squat flame-shape, flattened sprays of greeny-gold foliage, fertile well-drained soil not drying badly in summer. ○

Dwarf lavender—edging plants, e.g., "Hidcote"
E 8-by-8-inch, plant in rows and clip after flowering, semiformal silvery edging with lavender flowers summer, well-drained soil. ○

Festuca glauca
E 6-by-12-inch, tufty clump, blue-leafed grass, well-drained soil. ○

Fragaria "Pink Panda"
E 6-by-8-inch, spreading, strawberry plant with pink flowers summer, most soils. ◐◗

Galium odoratum (sweet woodruff)
E 24-by-8-inch upright, scented leaves with small white flowers in spring, moist soil. ◗

Gaultheria procumbens (wintergreen)
E 4-inch-by-$3\frac{1}{4}$-foot, carpeter, red berries fall/winter, lime-free soil. ◗

Geranium (hardy cranesbill)—
compact type, e.g., "Ballerina", *endresii*
H 6-by-18-inch, domed clump, pink flowers all
summer, reasonably well-drained soil. ○◗

Golden marjoram
SE 6-by-12-inch, domed clump, gold foliage all
summer, well-drained soil. ○

Heaths—mixed colors
E 6-by-10-inch, clumps, purple, mauve, white, and
pink flowers summer or winter depending on
species, well-drained acid soil (winter flowering
heaths tolerate slightly alkaline soil) including
exposed sites. ○

Heuchera
E 12-by-12-inch, mounds, airy sprays of pink or red
flower mid-summer, reasonably well-drained soil. ○◗

Houttuynia cordata "Chameleon"
H 8-by-18-inch, spreading, red, cream, and green
variegated ivy-like leaves, most soils including wet.
Also good in containers. ○◗

Hyacinths
H 9-by-6-inch, upright, highly scented spikes of
flower spring, fertile well-drained soil. ○

Lamium maculatum
H 4-by-18-inch, spreading mats, dead-nettle foliage
in green, variegated, or silver foliage with white or
pink nettle flowers (plant doesn't sting), most soils
except very dry. ◗

Narcissus (daffodil)
H 12-by-12-inch, upright, golden flowers spring,
most soils except waterlogged. Dwarf varieties. ○◗

Nepeta mussinii (catmint)
H 12-by-18-inch, clumps, gray-green aromatic
foliage and lavender flowers late spring to late
summer, light well-drained soil. ○

Phlox subulata
E 6-inch upright, low-growing, rapidly spreading,
needle-shaped foliage. Star-shaped, white, pink, or
mauve flowers in early summer, well-drained soil of
low fertility. ○◗

Potentilla
D 2-by-2-foot, domed bushy shape, single flat-faced

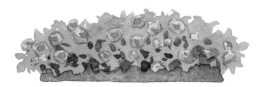

flowers in red, orange, yellow, or white early to late
summer, light well-drained soil. ○

Pulmonaria (lungwort)
H 12-by-18-inch, clumps, silver-white spotted
leaves and blue flowers spring, most soils. ●

Rockery plants—mixed
E+D various, carpeting, flowers over most of the
year, well-drained soil. ○

Rose—ground cover; orange, pink, or red
SE, 10-by-20-inch, carpeting, flowers all summer,
most soil specially heavier. ○

Rose—miniature
SE 8-by-8-inch, bushy shape, small flowers all
summer, rich well-drained soil, shelter—less hardy
than most roses. ○

Salad greens—various (red and green
lettuces, arugula, scallions, etc.)
A 8-inch, rows, russet and green shades, edible
crops for picking summer and fall, rich moist soil. ○

Snowdrops
H 4-by-2-inch, upright tufts, nodding white flowers
early spring, most soils. ◗●

Stachys lanata (*S. byzantina*)
(bunnies' ears, lamb's tongue)
SE 12-inch-by-2-foot, loose silvery carpet with
upright pale pink flower spikes mid to late summer,
well-drained soil. ○

Thymus—creeping
E 2-by-12-inch, mats, felted leaves, pink flowers late
spring and early summer plus aromatic foliage, well-

VITAL STATISTICS

A Annual flower, only present in summer;
B Biennial; **D** Deciduous; **E** Evergreen;
H Herbaceous; **SE** Semievergreen;
○ Sunny position ◗ Half-sunny position
● Shady position

drained soil. Good for cracks in paving. ○

Tulips—pink, red, white, or yellow
H 12-by-4-inch, upright, large flowers late spring,
light well-drained soil. ○

Vegetables—various,
e.g., carrots, cabbages, zucchini
A 16-inch, rows, edible crops for picking summer
and fall, rich moist soil. ○

Vinca (Periwinkle)
E 6-by-6½-foot spreading, single blue star-like flowers
late spring to late summer, most soils, variegated
foliage also available. ◗●

Viola labradorica
E 3-by-2-inch, bushy-rosette, mauve flowers
summer and purple-tinged foliage, most soils. ○●

Winter-flowering pansies
A 6-by-4-inch, upright clumps, large flat flower
"faces" in various colors all winter and spring, well-
drained soil, good with spring bulbs or in
containers. ○

*There are more than 265 plant cards in this pack.
In all instances, the plants are shown in bloom and
fully grown to represent the plant at its best.*

SOIL-TESTING KIT INSTRUCTIONS

Using a teaspoon, take a sample of soil from about 2-3 in below the surface. Remove any large particles and allow to dry.
Carefully open one capsule from the kit and pour contents into the smaller, testing chamber. Using the larger half of the empty capsule as a
measure, add two capsule-fuls of soil to the testing chamber. Fill with water, preferably distilled or rain water, to the dotted line. Close lid and
shake thoroughly. Allow to stand for a few minutes. Compare color against the chart to find the pH of your soil.

Immediately after use, dispose of test solutions down the sink. Remove color chart and wash all parts thoroughly in warm, soapy water.
Rinse and dry. Replace color chart. Store remaining capsules inside the container and keep in a cool dry place out of the reach of children.
Wash hands carefully after using the kit.

The photographs provided by The Garden Picture Library, London, are the copyright of the following photographers :
David Askham (p.20 twice), Linda Burgess (p. 2, 22, 27), Bob Challinor (p. 17), Kathy Charlton (p. 30), Densey Clyne (p. 33), Dennis Davis
(p. 34), David England (p. 25), Ron Evans (p. 17), Vaughan Fleming (p. 26), Nigel Francis (p. 25), John Glover (p. 8, 11, 24, 31, 36, 37 twice), Gil Hanly (p. 9),
Sunniva Harte (p. 25, 28), Neil Holmes (p. 6), Michele Lamontagne (p. 15, 20, 23, 32), Jane Legate (p. 6), Mayer/Le Scanff (p. 36), Zara McCalmont (p.14), Jerry Pavia (p.21), Joanne Pavia (p.9), Howard Rice (p.10, 24, 28), Gary Rogers (p. 31), J.S.Sira (p.18, 22), Ron Sutherland (p. 8, 14, 15, 29, 35 twice), Brigitte Thomas (p. 7, 10, 19, 23, 27), Juliette Wade
(p.10), Didier Willery (p.18), Steven Wooster (p. 7, 16, 32).

VIKING

Published by the Penguin Group, Penguin Books USA Inc, 375 Hudson Street, New York, New York 10014, USA
First published in Great Britain by George Weidenfeld & Nicolson Limited
Copyright © George Weidenfeld & Nicolson Limited, 1996
All rights reserved

Pack concept: Charles Ensor
Text: Sue Phillips
Illustrations: Ian Sidaway
Pack photographs: Chas Wilder
Design and color reproduction: Blackjacks Ltd
Editing: First Edition Translations Ltd., and Cathy Meeus
US plant consultant: John Elsley of Wayside Gardens plant catalogs
(Hodges, S.C. 29695-0001)

ISBN 0-670-86963-5

CIP data available

Printed in Hong Kong and bound in China

Without limiting the rights under copyright reserved above, no part of this publication may be reproduced, stored in or
introduced into a retrieval system, or transmitted, in any form or by any means (electronic, mechanical, photocopying,
recording, or otherwise), without the prior written permission of both the copyright owner and the above publisher of this
book.